The media's watching Vault!
Here's a sampling of our coverage.

"For those hoping to climb the ladder of success, [Vault's] insights are priceless."
– *Money magazine*

"The best place on the web to prepare for a job search."
– *Fortune*

"[Vault guides] make for excellent starting points for job hunters and should be purchased by academic libraries for their career sections [and] university career centers."
– *Library Journal*

"The granddaddy of worker sites."
– *U.S. News and World Report*

"A killer app."
– *New York Times*

One of Forbes' 33 "Favorite Sites"
– *Forbes*

"To get the unvarnished scoop, check out Vault."
– *Smart Money Magazine*

"Vault has a wealth of information about major employers and job-searching strategies as well as comments from workers about their experiences at specific companies."
– *The Washington Post*

"Vault has become the go-to source for career preparation."
– *Crain's New York Business*

"Vault [provides] the skinny on working conditions at all kinds of companies from current and former employees."
– *USA Today*

VAULT
> the most trusted name in career information™

VAULT CAREER GUIDE TO
PHARMACEUTICAL
SALES & MARKETING

CAROLE S. MOUSSALLI
AND THE STAFF OF VAULT

For information about permission to reproduce selections from this book, contact Vault Inc., 150 W. 22nd St., 5th Floor, New York, NY 10011, (212) 366-4212.

Library of Congress CIP Data is available.

ISBN 1-58131-386-1

Printed in the United States of America

ACKNOWLEDGMENTS

Acknowledgments from Carole Moussalli

I would like to express a sincere thanks to the individuals who have provided insights and comments to the career roles described in this complex, dynamic, and rapidly changing industry. Their contributions lend authenticity to the volume and provide a roadmap for those embarking on biopharmaceutical careers. I had promised and now honor the need for anonymity. I can only thank them collectively.

I especially want to thank my editor, Matthew Thornton, for his thoughtful comments and meticulous editorial support. And thank you also to the dedicated Vault staff for ensuring the manuscript meets the highest standards.

Finally, for their unflagging support, advice, and patience, I am particularly indebted to my aunt Linda Sayegh, my father Francois Moussalli, and my sister Dr. Clarice Moussalli, for without whose relationships, the journey would not have been as much fun.

Vault Acknowledgments

We are extremely grateful to Vault's entire staff for all their help in the editorial, production and marketing processes. Vault also would like to acknowledge the support of our investors, clients, employees, family, and friends. Thank you!

Table of Contents

Visit Vault at **www.vault.com** for insider company profiles, expert advice,
career message boards, expert resume reviews, the Vault Job Board and more.

V/\ULT CAREER LIBRARY   vii

Visit Vault at **www.vault.com** for insider company profiles, expert advice,
career message boards, expert resume reviews, the Vault Job Board and more.

VAULT CAREER LIBRARY

ix

Final Analysis   167

APPENDIX   169

Introduction

What's in a name: Big Pharma, Big Biotech and Biopharma

Strictly speaking, the term "pharmaceuticals" refers to medicines composed of small, synthetically produced molecules, which are sold by large, fully integrated drug manufacturers. The largest of these players—companies like Pfizer, GlaxoSmithKline and Merck—as well as a handful of others are referred to as "Big Pharma" because they are huge research, development, and manufacturing concerns with subsidiaries all over the globe. Indeed, Big Pharma is where over 50% of the industry's sales are generated. Big Pharma is responsible for all those television commercials urging us to contact our doctors if we suspect we suffer from acid reflux disease or social anxiety disorder. Yet despite life-saving, cancer-fighting drugs and significant corporate philanthropy, Big Pharma's recent product recalls and safety testing troubles (Vioxx and Celebrex) have made it the industry many have come to love to hate.

Before we help you chart a marketing career in the industry, we should point out that both the scope of players and the types of products the industry produces are moving targets. This is because the pharmaceutical and biotech industries are gradually integrating into one biopharmaceutical industry. Here's what you should know about this dynamic restructuring.

"Fully integrated"

Most biotechs are small research-oriented companies dedicated to applying genetics to curing a multitude of diseases, from Alzheimer's to multiple sclerosis. A handful of companies—such as Amgen, Genentech and Chiron—have broken through the rest of the pack to become "fully integrated" like their Big Pharma cousins. The term "fully integrated" means that they manufacture as well as sell their own products. These "products" are proteins, which need to be administered via injections, since they are very large molecules compared to the synthetic molecules Big Pharma sells. The largest biotechs are actually mid-size pharmaceutical companies in the way they function and are sometimes called "Big Biotech."

Visit Vault at **www.vault.com** for insider company profiles, expert advice, career message boards, expert resume reviews, the Vault Job Board and more.

VAULT CAREER LIBRARY   1

As for the largest Big Pharma players, most are either gobbling up small biotechs through outright acquisitions or, alternatively, are entering licensing agreements. This has been happening over the last decade, and is likely to continue throughout the rest of this decade, since it is increasingly difficult to find innovative new drugs through traditional science. In fact, innovation is the industry's biggest current challenge. Companies are using acquisitions and alliances to round out their product pipelines and meet investor expectations. Big drug manufacturers can now claim to research, manufacture and sell both types of drugs: synthetic small molecules (or old chemistry) and injectable large molecules (or biologics). What this means to you is that you should include the largest biotechs as well as the largest traditional pharmaceuticals in your plans when thinking about a marketing career. And this is good news since it increases the number of players and potential employers.

Organizational structures

Pharmaceutical companies are generally organized around the "blockbuster" model, i.e., they derive most of their sales and profits from a handful of broadly acting drugs, which are mass-marketed to a broad patient population by a network of sales representatives, or "detail" people. This is the same model that brought Vioxx to the market and it is increasingly under attack. By industry consensus, a "blockbuster" is a drug whose annual revenues reach or exceed $1 billion.

The biotech firms, on the other hand, tend to be organized around smaller franchises, i.e., their products are targeted to small patient populations with rare genetic diseases. Their biologics are sold by specialty sales representatives, who often have a relatively high degree of scientific knowledge. Because of this focus, biotech products are often referred to as specialty pharmaceuticals. To complicate matters, some biologics reach blockbuster status with respect to their revenues, since they are usually much more expensive than synthetics. Considering that some biologics cost $10,000 per patient per year, you would need a mere 100,000 patients to reach $1 billion in revenues. Compare this to the millions of patients who ingest small molecule drugs like Prozac or Viagra.

Introducing "biopharma"

The dividing line between the pharma and biotech industries will continue to blur. That leaves us with the problem of how to refer to the emerging industry. We'll be using the term "Biopharma" to include both types of products. As it turns out, most companies require some experience in pharma sales before permitting someone to move into specialty sales. That's a significant factor in charting your career. Both Big Pharma companies as well as biotechs can have specialty products. The distinction is that biotech products are exclusively specialty products, whereas Big Pharma—which has a broader product offering—has products targeted at primary care physicians and products aimed at specialists.

One final comment about the industry's products: both synthetic or biologic drugs are directed toward the treatment of disease. The industry refers to this broad category as 'therapeutics,' since these drugs have a therapeutic effect on the disease condition. But the biopharma industry also has another category of products focused on helping medical scientists more accurately determine (or diagnose) a disease condition from a patient presenting multiple, often difficult-to-interpret symptoms. These products are called 'diagnostics' and may come from biologic sources. Often, diagnostic agents (they are NOT called drugs) are used in conjunction with a medical device or instrument. A good example is the diagnostic imaging agent technetium 99m, which helps MRI machines create clearer cross-sections of the human body.

Use the Internet's
MOST TARGETED
job search tools.

Vault Job Board

Target your search by industry, function, and experience level, and find the job openings that you want.

VaultMatch Resume Database

Vault takes match-making to the next level: post your resume and customize your search by industry, function, experience and more. We'll match job listings with your interests and criteria and e-mail them directly to your inbox.

VAULT
> the most trusted name in career information™

THE SCOOP

Overview of the Biopharmaceutical Industry

CHAPTER 1

The Global Biopharmaceutical Industry

The global industry is dominated by three major market segments: North America is the largest and comprises 49% of the total market, Europe is second with some 28%, and Japan third at 11% in 2003 sales. Although these combined markets account for 78% of global sales, the remaining emerging market segments—Other Asian, Africa, and Australia and Latin America—are growing rapidly.

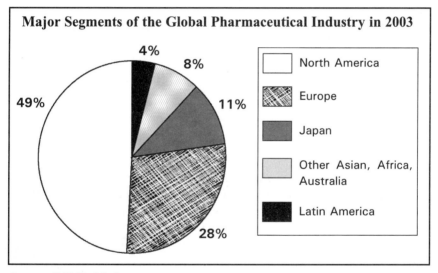

Major Segments of the Global Pharmaceutical Industry in 2003

- North America
- Europe
- Japan
- Other Asian, Africa, Australia
- Latin America

Source: IMS Health, Inc.

Although the industry is dominated by a handful of super-large companies, the global industry is actually highly fragmented. Over 2,000 pharmaceutical and biotech companies exist worldwide. In the top tier are the large, multinational companies that dominate the market or Big Pharma. In the middle tier are the specialty companies. Many large companies have tended to absorb second-tier companies before they can grow enough to pose a competitive threat. That trend has a contracting effect on the number of firms. The opposite happens on the third and lowest tier, which is composed of an ever-increasing group of start-ups mostly focused on discovery research.

Visit Vault at **www.vault.com** for insider company profiles, expert advice, career message boards, expert resume reviews, the Vault Job Board and more.

VAULT CAREER LIBRARY

7

According to IMS Health, Inc., a healthcare research and information company, as recently as 1998, the global pharmaceutical market was valued at $280 billion. By 2003, total global sales had grown 9% over 2002 levels to $492 billion or nearly half a trillion dollars! This figure was derived from retail sales in major global markets. This astonishing growth over a five-year period reflects the increasing role of pharmaceuticals as a first-line treatment option for many disease conditions in the developed world. The term "first-line" means that physicians opt to prescribe a pharmaceutical first in lieu of a more invasive procedure, such as surgery. In some cancers, physicians now have the option of recommending a tumor-shrinking drug, for example, before surgery so as to minimize the level of invasiveness to the body. This has resulted in less trauma to body tissues and discomfort to the patient.

2003 Sales Growth in Major Markets

Market	Growth (%)
North America	11
Europe	8
Asia (excluding Japan), Africa and Australia	12
Latin America	6
Japan	3

Source: IMS Health, Inc.

Economic activity is concentrated in both diagnostic agents and therapeutic drugs. In 2000, the highest selling 20 drugs generated sales revenues of $100 billion or roughly 50% of total sales of the top 500 drugs. In 2002, 58 products each generated sales over $1 billion. Reflecting the stress-ridden, developed world's disease vulnerabilities, the most profitable products treated heart disease, gastric distress, mood and mental disorders, and inflammatory conditions.

Worldwide 2003 Sales of Top Therapeutic Areas

Rank	Therapeutic Area	Billion $
1	Cholesterol and triglyceride reducers	26.1
2	Antiulcer medications	24.3
3	Antidepressants	19.5
4	Antirheumatic non-steroids	12.4
5	Antipsychotics	12.2
6	Calcium antagonists	10.8
7	Erythropoietin products	10.1
8	Antiepileptics	9.4
9	Oral antidiabetics	9.0
10	Cephalosporins and combinations	8.3

Source: IMS Health, Inc.

The U.S. Pharmaceutical Industry

The U.S. pharmaceutical industry is comprised of approximately 100 companies, according to the Pharmaceutical Research and Manufacturers of America (PhRMA), a leading industry trade and lobbying organization, with the top 10 companies referred to as Big Pharma. This does not include biotech companies, which number approximately 325 publicly traded companies, with hundreds more private, discovery research-oriented firms. The U.S. drug market is concentrated—Big Pharma accounted for 60% of total retail sales in 2003, according to IMS Health, Inc.

The U.S. has not only the largest pharmaceutical market in the world but also the only one without government price controls. This is a consequence of the privately owned system prevalent in the U.S. and a strong industry lobby, which has resisted government incursions into its market-based pricing. On the other hand, developed economies with universal healthcare access (European Union, UK, Japan) exert stringent controls on the prices companies can charge. A big consequence is that, with thin profit margins, the incentive for innovation is curbed, and former leaders, especially in the EU (German and French companies, in particular) lost the lead in innovation in the 1990s. Standard & Poor's expects the U.S. to continue to be the largest of the top 10 pharmaceutical markets for the foreseeable future, as well as the fastest growing.

Although pharmaceutical companies are scattered throughout the continental United States, the industry is geographically concentrated in the Mid-Atlantic States (New York, New Jersey, and Pennsylvania) and on the West Coast in California. A handful of companies can also be found in Massachusetts, Illinois, and North Carolina. New Jersey is the heart of the industry and has by far the largest number of companies within a single state.

Top 10 Big Pharma Companies in 2003

Rank	Therapeutic Area	Billion $
1	Pfizer	47.08
2	GlaxoSmithKline	30.78
3	Merck	22.52
4	Johnson & Johnson	22.18
5	Novartis	20.25
6	AstraZeneca	19.21
7	Aventis	17.02
8	Bristol-Myers Squibb	15.69
9	Roche	15.23
10	Abbott	13.27

Source: IMS Health, Inc. and S&P Industry Surveys

Top Ten Prescription Drugs Worldwide in 2003

Drug	Company	Therapeutic Area	Sales (billion $)
Lipitor	Pfizer	Cholesterol Lowering	10.3
Zocor	Merck	Cholesterol Lowering	6.1
Zyprexa	Lilly	Anti-psychotic	4.8
Novarsc	Pfizer	Anti-hypertensive	4.5
Epogen	Amgen	Red blood cell stimulant	4.0
Ogastro/Prevacid	TAP Pharma-Abbott	Anti-ulcer	4.0
Nexium	AstraZeneca	Anti-ulcer	3.8
Plavix	Sanofi Pharmaceuticals	Blood clot inhibitor	3.7
Seretide	GlaxoSmithKline	Anti-asthmatic	3.7
Zoloft	Pfizer	Anti-depressant	3.4

Sources: IMS Health, Inc. and S&P Industry Surveys

The Federal Government's Role

Since the early 20th Century, the Federal Government has played an increasingly active role in defining industry standards and regulating commercial activity. The U.S. pharmaceutical industry has had the tightest standards of safety in the world.

In 1906, Congress passed the Pure Food and Drug Act, which required that drugs meet official standards of strength and purity and that a drug's ingredients be accurately described on the drug's label. In 1938, after about 100 deaths following consumption of the elixir sulfanilamide (now used in automotive anti-freeze), Congress passed the Food, Drug, and Cosmetic Act, which required drug manufacturers to submit evidence of a product's safety, to clearly label a product's contents, give instructions for administration, and list the drug's possible side effects. A new agency, the Food and Drug Administration (FDA), was created to ensure industry compliance.

In the 1960s, Congress further strengthened safety requirements with the 1962 passage of the Kefauver-Harris Act, which gave the FDA greater control over prescription drugs and required more comprehensive evidence of a drug's safety, efficacy and adverse reactions on advertising materials. Kefauver-Harris also required that manufacturing be according to specified "good manufacturing practices" (GMP) guidelines and that the FDA periodically inspect manufacturing facilities.

In the 1980s, Congress expanded the scope of the industry with the 1983 passage of the Orphan Drug Act, which made research on drugs for rare diseases with small patient populations (under 200,000) economically viable by granting exclusive marketing rights to the manufacturer. By early 2004, over 1,300 experimental products had received orphan status from the FDA, with 250 already approved. In 1984, the Hatch-Waxman Act broadened the availability of generics and allowed greater patent protection for new drugs to compensate for time lost during the FDA approval process. In 1988, the Prescription Drug Marketing Act established requirements for distribution of samples and created safeguards against the sale of substandard or counterfeit drugs.

The FDA in the 1990s

In the 1990s, the regulatory role of the FDA became murkier. In 1991, the FDA accelerated the review of drugs for life-threatening diseases, a move which many applauded and which helped bring treatments for HIV/AIDS to market faster. In 1992, Congress passed the Prescription Drug User Fees Act (PDUFA), which required manufacturers to pay user fees to enhance FDA staff and resources for faster approvals of new drugs. It seemed like a good idea at the time, but in hindsight, this legislation fundamentally changed the relationship between the FDA and the industry, effectively making the manufacturers the clients of their regulatory agency. With the hindsight of the Merck recall of one of its leading revenue generators, the painkiller Vioxx, industry critics charged that the FDA compromised itself with a conflict of interest, acting to expedite the approval of the of this drug at the expense of the public's safety. In early 2005, concerns over other products, such as Pfizer's Celebrex, have further highlighted safety concerns and brought the debate over drug safety evaluation public.

Matters were further complicated with the 1997 easing of FDA restrictions on direct-to-consumer (DTC) advertising of prescription drugs. By 2004, the industry was spending $3 billion on DTC advertising with greater spending likely in future years. But the value of that aspect of industry activity has also been questioned and, by early 2005, a lively debate is likely to continue on how drugs are marketed. The upshot is that reform is inevitable and is likely to affect a number of areas within the marketing function.

Post-Millennium: Vaccines and "blockbusters"

In the years since the turn of the millennium, the industry responded with characteristic largesse after the 2001 terrorist attacks in New York and Washington, DC, with contributions of cash, medicines, equipment, and personnel. The industry has also been working with the federal government to define a defense strategy against bioterrorist threats. In 2003, industry trade group PhRMA launched a Web site (http://www.helpingpatients.org) as an information resource for individual member companies' patient assistance programs. In late 2004, the industry again contributed millions of dollars in cash and medicines to the tsunami-devastated countries of South Asia. However, the same players, for pricing and profit reasons, did not have enough flu vaccine available during the 2004-05 flu season.

The biopharmaceutical industry entered the second half of the 2000s with controversy and hope alike. The role of the FDA in verifying the safety of a drug prior to granting marketing approval is likely to be redefined in the next several years. The business model that created the flu vaccine shortage will also have to be revamped, especially with the onus of avian flu mutating to human-to-human transfer. Briefly, flu vaccine shortages arose as a result of the dearth of manufacturers: only two made the drug, and one, Chiron, saw its facility in the UK shut down for safety concerns. That more companies do not make vaccines is due to low prices, no profit margin and high potential liability, a toxic economic mix from which most companies have self-selected out of the vaccine industry. Since the drumbeat over avian flu has intensified, limited manufacturing is no longer an option. The Bush administration has met with industry leaders to address the issue.

The "blockbuster" model is coming under intense scrutiny, since, with millions of prescriptions, the tiny percentage but significant number of people with adverse effects (e.g., heart attacks from painkillers) can lead to devastating social and economic consequences. Despite these cautionary circumstances, innovation is likely to come from the biotech branch of the industry, with dozens of anti-cancer drugs at different stages of development and other products for chronic and life threatening conditions.

Innovation: The Industry's Main Driver

Biopharmaceuticals is an industry driven by innovation and technological advances. According to PhRMA, between 1993 and 2003, the industry spent over $200 billion on research and development. The fruit of this investment was over 363 new therapeutics, biologics, and vaccines, which were approved by the FDA to treat over 150 diseases and conditions. During the same period, the industry obtained FDA approval to market an annual average of 32 new medicines. In recent years, the industry marketed 27 products in 2000, 24 in 2001, 26 in 2002 and 35 in 2003, according to PhRMA's 2004 Industry Profile.

In 2003, PhRMA reports that research-based pharmaceutical companies invested $33.2 billion on research and development of new drugs. This figure represents about 17.7% of domestic sales and is higher than R&D expenditures in any other industry. Furthermore, this figure is higher than either $24 billion—the entire budget of the National Institutes of Health—or the R&D investment of the international pharmaceutical industry. In 2003, the FDA approved 21 new drugs and 14 new biologics to prevent or treat Alzheimer's disease, cancer, HIV infection, asthma, influenza, pneumonia, and psoriasis.

Profit and loss

Yet for all that investment, industry executives point out that the costs of research are not recouped for most of the products that reach the market.

Visit Vault at www.vault.com for insider company profiles, expert advice, career message boards, expert resume reviews, the Vault Job Board and more.

VAULT CAREER LIBRARY

13

According to PhRMA, only 3 out of 10 marketed products generate enough revenue to recoup average development costs. That means that the other 7 do not recover their costs. A further implication is that the healthy profits that have made pharmaceuticals so attractive to the investment community are generated largely from the handful of blockbusters that are mass-marketed at a premium. In recent years, American consumers have come to understand that we pay more for our prescription drugs than any other group on the planet.

But if consumers are howling, the industry is groaning under the gargantuan cost of bringing a new product to market. In a June 2001 study, the Boston Consulting Group (BCG) estimated that it cost the industry $880 million to develop and market a new therapeutic drug. In May 2003, the Tufts Center for the Study of Drug Development, a non-profit academic research group, estimated that it costs the industry, on average, approximately $897 million to bring a new drug to the market (in 2000 dollars). This figure includes R&D costs of the product itself, advertising and promotion costs, the costs of developing non-profitable drugs. That figure should reach over $900 billion in 2004.

These prohibitive costs are sobering in light of the essential nature of innovation. According to Robert Essner, Chairman of PhRMA, "To see the fragility of innovation, one need only look at Europe, where rigid price controls have dried up pharmaceutical innovation. The region once was the 'world's medicine chest,' but during the 1990s was overtaken by the U.S. as the leading site for pharmaceutical innovation. Today, global pharmaceutical companies spend 40 percent more on research and development in the United States than in Europe. Just 10 years ago, the opposite was true; industry was spending 50 percent more in Europe than in the States."

Tactics for boosting productivity

Because of the staggering development costs, the industry uses several tactics to boost R&D productivity. Companies create combination products with enhanced efficacy and convenience to the consumer. A good example is the drug Zytorin, a combination of Merck's cholesterol-lowering Zocor and Schering-Plough's Zetia, another cholesterol drug. Zytorin offers greater efficacy than either drug used alone because it combines the action of Zocor, which inhibits cholesterol production in the liver, with that of Zetia, which blocks the absorption of cholesterol in the gastrointestinal tract.

Companies apply for patent life extensions and identify new uses or new indications to older, existing drugs. The approval of new indications effectively extends the life of a patent on a drug and brings a new product to market at a fraction of the cost of developing a brand new medicine. The overall effect is to broaden the sales base and extend the period of market exclusivity, both factors that support profit margins on a product. Anti-cancer medications have been applied effectively here. Lilly's pancreatic cancer drug, Gemzar, initially approved in 1996, was also approved for non-small cell lung cancer in 1998. Work is continuing on obtaining approvals for use against bladder and ovarian cancers.

For each new indication approved, a company must submit a supplemental new drug application (sNDA), which demonstrates the safety and efficacy of the drug for the new indication. Anti-depressants, such as Zoloft, Paxil, and Celexa, have also been approved for anxiety and panic disorder, effectively broadening the market for this classification. The anti-hypertensive drugs, Inspra, Cozaar, and Norvasc have also been approved for congestive heart failure.

The most recent—and undoubtedly controversial—productivity-boosting tactic has been the outsourcing of research and development and some clinical trial functions to cheaper labor markets, most notably in China. Although Chinese labor is certainly less expensive, time will tell if this tactic proves effective.

Evolution of Innovation in Biopharmaceuticals: 1993-2003

Year	Disease or Condition	Treatment
1993	Alzheimer's Disease	Acetylcholinesterase inhibitors
1995	Diabetes	Biguanides, alpha-glucosidase inhibitors
	HIV/AIDS	Protease inhibitors
	High blood pressure	Angiotensin-II antagonists
1996	HIV/AIDS	Non-nucleoside reverse transcriptase inhibitors
1997	Parkinson's Disease	Second generation dopamine agonists
	Diabetes	Meglitinides, thiazolidinediones
1998	Parkinson's Disease	COMT inhibitors
	Rheumatoid Arthritis Alzheimer's Disease	Biological response modifiers, new disease-modifying anti-rheumatic drug, COX-2 inhibitors
2000		Cholinesterase inhibitors

Visit Vault at **www.vault.com** for insider company profiles, expert advice, career message boards, expert resume reviews, the Vault Job Board and more.

VAULT CAREER LIBRARY

15

Year	Disease or Condition	Treatment
	Diabetes	D-phenylalanine derivatives, two new types of insulin
2001	HIV/AIDS	Nucleotide analogue reverse transcriptase inhibitors
2002	High blood cholesterol	Absorption inhibitors
	High blood pressure	Selective aldosterone receptor antagonists
2003	HIV/AIDS	Fusion inhibitors

Source: PhRMA

On the positive side, the FDA increased the number of New Molecular Entities (NMEs) approved in 2003 and 2004 and cleared approvals for new indications of existing drugs. Twenty-one NMEs were approved in 2003, up from 17 in 2002. The term, 'new molecular entity' is a term used by the FDA to refer, as broadly and generically as possible, to molecules (either small or large, synthetic or biologic), which may become approved after meeting all safety and efficacy hurdles.

Recently Approved New Molecular Entities (NMEs)

Company	Trade Name	Therapeutic Area	Approval Date
Bristol Myers Squibb	Entecavir	Chronic Hepatitis B	March 29, 2005
Amylin	Symlin	Type 1 and 2 diabetes	March 16, 2005
Sepracor	Lunesta	Sleep disorders	December 15, 2004
Eli Lilly	Cymbalta	Antidepressant	August 03, 2004
Amgen	Sensipar	Hyperparathyroidism	March 8, 2004

Sources: Data from S&P Industry Surveys

Potential Blockbusters

Company	Trade Name	Therapeutic Area	Approval Date
Bristol-Myers Squibb and Otsuka America Pharmaceutical, Inc.	Abilify (aripiprazole)	Antipsychotic	Over $1 billion
Pfizer	Inspra (eplerenone)	Lowers blood pressure following heart failure	$500 million
Abbott Laboratories	Humira (adalimumab)	Psoriartic Arthritis	Over $800 million
Eli Lilly & Co.	Strattera (atomoxetine HCl)	Attention Deficit / Hyperactivity Disorder (ADHD)	Over $500 million
Merck and Schering-Plough	Zetia (ezetimibe)	Lowers LDL (bad) cholesterol	Over $1.2 billion

Sources: Standard & Poor's Industry Surveys, June 26, 2003.

The Current Environment

The complex domain of health economics has become increasingly politicized in recent years. Basically, sales revenues are increasing since more people are taking more drugs to treat more conditions. Although some critics decry America as overmedicated, others point out that people are taking more medicines because drugs are evolving as a first-line of therapy for many conditions and, however costly, are much more economical than aggressive treatments, such as surgery.

But since the beginning of this decade, sales growth has been accompanied with downward pressure on profit margins, due to increased price resistance, generic competition, and concerns for safety. Total U.S. drug sales (branded and generic) increased 11.5% in 2003 to $216.4 billion. As a class, prescription drug sales rose 15% in 2002, over 13% in 2003 and just below 13% in 2004, according to the Center of Medicare and Medicaid Services (CMS), the federal agency that manages these programs and estimates national healthcare costs and expenditures.

Visit Vault at **www.vault.com** for insider company profiles, expert advice, career message boards, expert resume reviews, the Vault Job Board and more.

VAULT CAREER LIBRARY

17

Growth factors

Factors accounting for growth include the continuing strength of generic drugs and biotech products, with branded pharmaceuticals showing more limited single digit growth. Generics and biotech products posted sales gains of over 20% in 2003. Oncology (anti-cancer) and autoimmune therapeutics products contributed significantly to this gain. Growth in branded pharmaceuticals slowed due to erosion of sales in hormone replacement therapy (HRT), increased purchasing of drugs from Canada, a mild flu season, and losses from patent expirations. Slowing sales of HRT is particularly significant, since women in the Baby Boom generation are currently in their menopausal years. Despite industry efforts, many women have resisted HRT, due to concerns about evidence of association with cancer, and weight gain, among others. Given the tens of millions of women in this cohort, resistance to HRT has created a drag in overall sales volumes.

Big Pharma earnings grew about 10% in 2003 and 2004, a far cry from the high double-digits of the 1990s. Sources of downward pressure on profit margins include government-mandated price rollbacks and rebates, greater use of reference pricing throughout Europe, and increased use of parallel trade. Reference pricing limits reimbursement to the least expensive drug in a given classification. For example, if three drugs have three different prices, governments reimburse companies based on the least expensive drug. Parallel trade is the practice of buying drugs in cheaper markets—such as Spain and Greece—and reselling them in higher priced markets—such as Germany and Britain.

CMS has put drug spending in perspective by breaking down the healthcare dollar. The prescription drug component in the chart below includes branded prescription drugs, generic copies, and pharmacy expenses. Combined total sales comprise just 10% of total healthcare dollars. The industry loves to point this out, saying that for every dollar the U.S. spends on healthcare, pharmaceuticals account for a mere 10 cents and that surgery and hospital expenses consume a far greater share. What is significant to remember, however, is that, according to S&P analysts, growth rates for prescription drug outlays are likely to remain the highest of all components of national health outlays. And this is what has had consumers howling, politicians paying attention, and the industry scrambling.

Breakdown of Healthcare Dollar (2002)

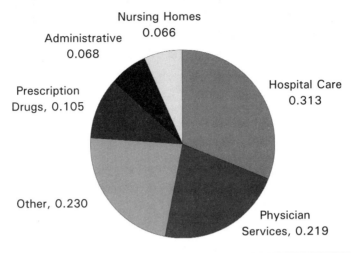

Nursing Homes 0.066

Administrative 0.068

Prescription Drugs, 0.105

Hospital Care 0.313

Other, 0.230

Physician Services, 0.219

Hospital Care	Physician	Other
Prescription Drugs	Administrative Costs	Nursing Homes

Prescription Drug Sales in 2002

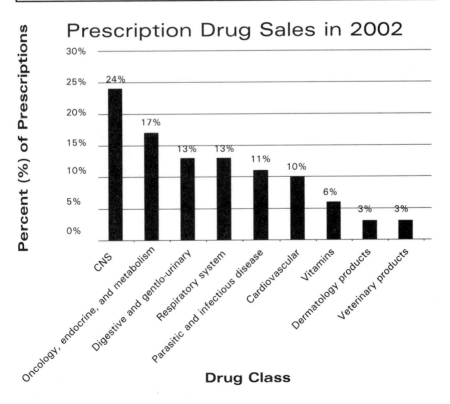

Percent (%) of Prescriptions

- CNS — 24%
- Oncology, endocrine, and metabolism — 17%
- Digestive and gentlo-urinary — 13%
- Respiratory system — 13%
- Parasitic and infectious disease — 11%
- Cardiovascular — 10%
- Vitamins — 6%
- Dermatology products — 3%
- Veterinary products — 3%

Drug Class

Visit Vault at **www.vault.com** for insider company profiles, expert advice,
career message boards, expert resume reviews, the Vault Job Board and more.

V/\ULT CAREER LIBRARY

19

The pharmaceutical market in the U.S. is likely to experience both positive and negative growth trends. Positive growth factors include an aging population, longer life span, a relatively free market, aggressive direct-to-consumer (DTC) campaigns and innovation either from in-house R&D or through alliances. Negative growth trends include pricing pressures from both managed care and government and patent expirations that lead to the broader availability of cheaper generics. Standard & Poor's estimates that the net effect of these trends is to keep sales growth in branded pharmaceuticals in the high single digits (about 8 to 9%) through the mid-2000s. Although this is generally good for a mature industry, it is not as attractive as the double-digit growth seen in the 1990s.

Managed Care: A Bigger Player

Managed care organizations (MCOs) are increasingly picking up the tab for prescription drugs in the U.S. Examples according to size include WellPoint Health Networks, UnitedHealth Group, Aetna, Inc., CIGNA, and Humana. According to IMS Health, in 2003, MCOs accounted for 73% of new prescriptions, an increase from 42% in 1994. Consumers paid for only 14% of prescriptions, down from 44% over the same period, with Medicare's share remaining unchanged at 13%. Managed care organizations have been moving aggressively to contain prescription drug costs.

Tactics MCOs use to contain prescription drug costs include bargaining power to obtain discounts for bulk purchases, incentives to members to use less expensive generics when available, restrictive formularies, and utilization of three-tier formularies. The term 'formulary' refers to the list of drugs approved by the MCO for dispensation to its subscribers. Approval of a drug into a formulary ensures a steady supply of end consumers. In the three-tier pricing structure, generics have lowest co-payment, branded formulary drugs have higher co-payment, and branded non-listed drugs the highest co-payment. The three-tier system is perhaps the most efficient of these tactics and is offered by approximately two-thirds of health plans. The co-payment structure is typically $10 for generics, $20 for branded formulary drugs, and $30 to $35 for branded non-formulary drugs.

Big Pharma companies usually maintain national accounts with MCOs and assign experienced sales personnel to manage them. These positions are contrasted with the standard sales rep positions, which focus on specific geographic areas and are more accessible early in your career.

Controversy at the Food and Drug Administration (FDA)

In the beginning of 2005, the FDA was under attack for expediting drug approvals at the expense of patient safety and Congress was reviewing the agency's process as well as its relationship to the industry. With the September 2004 recall of Merck's Vioxx and the scaling down of promotion of Pfizer's Celebrex in response to increased risk of heart attacks after extended use of the two Cox-2 inhibitors, the industry is as much on the defensive as the agency charged with regulating its activities. The problems around the Cox-2 inhibitors called into question practices put into place in the 1990s.

The most significant is the expedited review. It currently takes approximately 24 months for the FDA to review and approve a drug for marketing. Top analysts believe that, in the current environment, regulators are likely to ask drug companies to conduct more clinical trials over a longer period of time and in a broader population of patients so as to better detect possible adverse effects. That would help solve the safety issue, but at a price. A tougher FDA could translate into upward price pressure for drugs, something American consumers are resisting more and more tenaciously. This would happen if the FDA mandates longer clinical trials for larger patient populations, which would add to the cost of bringing drugs to market. Cheaper drugs for aging consumers living on fixed incomes present an attractive notion. But consider that, according to a Merrill Lynch study, each month that a drug spends under review represents $41.7 million in lost revenue. With profit margins slimming down and productivity from investment in R&D also slowing, your task as a pharmaceutical marketer is indeed challenging.

Yet the industry continues to turn out both therapeutics and biologics, with the sizzle likely to come from the latter, as the two-decade-long investment in biotech is poised to produce a plethora of new products across many disease conditions, especially cancer. How these new products get to market and under what new constraints is a story yet to be written.

Visit Vault at **www.vault.com** for insider company profiles, expert advice, career message boards, expert resume reviews, the Vault Job Board and more.

VAULT CAREER LIBRARY   21

Examples of New Therapeutics Approved in 2003 and 2004

Drug (trade name)	Therapeutic area	Impact on Patient
Lyrica	Pain management	Helps treat persistent nerve pain
Aloxi™(palonosetron HCl)	Prevents chemotherapy related nausea and vomiting	Helps cancer patients prevent chemotherapy-related nausea and vomiting during treatment day and for several days thereafter in cases where current anti-nausea medication is not effective.
Boniva®(ibandronate sodium)	Osteoperosis in postmenopausal women	Helps current 8 million women currently diagnosed with osteoporosis, a figure expected to increase as the number of postmenopausal women increases.
Cialis®) (tadalafil) Levitra® (vardenafil HCl)	Erectile dysfunction	Cialis®) is active for up to 36 hours. Up to 50% of men over the age of 40 suffer from this problem.
Reyataz® (atazanavir sulfate)	HIV infection combined with other drugs	As a protease inhibitor, Reyataz disables the enzyme that promotes viral maturation.
Velcade™ (bortezomib)	Multiple myeloma (cancer of the blood)	Disrupts growth and survival of cancer cells; first such treatment in 10 years.

Sources: PhRMA

Examples of New Biologics Approved in 2003 and 2004

Biologics (trade name)	Therapeutic area	Impact on Patient
Clolar®	Leukemia	Cancer drug for children and young adults with leukemia who don't respond to standard chemotherapy
Amevive® (alefacept)	Psoriasis	Targets underlying cause of disease— immune system dysfunction—which afflicts millions of Americans.
Bexxar® (tositumomab and iodine I-131 tositumomab)	Cancer therapy for follicular non-Hodgkin's lymphoma	Bexxar® helps the immune system initiate a response to this type of cancer.
FluMist™ (influenze virus vaccine line, intranasal)	Influenza	Treatment option for the 17 to 50 million people annually who come down with the flu. It is the first needle-free option for flu vaccination.
Xolair® (omalizumab)	Asthma	Targets underlying cause of asthma. PhRMA estimates that total costs of asthma are approximately $14 billion in 1998.

Sources: PhRMA

Visit Vault at **www.vault.com** for insider company profiles, expert advice, career message boards, expert resume reviews, the Vault Job Board and more.

VAULT CAREER LIBRARY   23

Biopharmaceutical Industry Trends

CHAPTER 2

Demographic Trends Favor Growth

Three major demographic trends in the developed world—aging Baby Boomers, increased life expectancy, and increased incidence of chronic diseases—make for ideal conditions for growth.

Aging Baby Boomers

According to the U.S. Census Bureau's Global Population Profile: 2002, the global cohort of people aged 65 and older will grow 89% during the 2002-2025 period—from 440 million people to 833 million people. Total global population is expected to rise only 26% during that same period. Moreover, expected growth is likely to occur in the developing world, where birthrates are higher and birth control methods less widely used than in more developed economies.

Approximately 293 million people live in the U.S. today, according to Census Bureau estimates. Bureau projections estimate that the over-65 segment will almost double from approximately 35.6 million in 2003 to about 62.6 million by 2025. This represents an increase in senior citizens from approximately 12.6% in 2003 to over 18.5% in 2025. While the overall population is expected to grow only 21%, seniors are projected to grow almost 80%. This same cohort also consumes approximately 40% of U.S. pharmaceutical products, according to S&P.

In addition, between 2005 and 2010, another segment, the 45-to-64 age group, will be the fastest growing cohort and will begin to consume prescription drugs with increased frequency. There were over 67 million people in this category in 2003.

Extended life expectancy

In 2001, life expectancy in the U.S. was 77.2 years, compared with 74.1 years in 1981 and 68.4 years in 1951, according to the Division of Vital Statistics (part of the National Center for Health Statistics). According to a UN report, American life expectancy is projected to reach 79.1 years between 2020 and

2025.   It's a virtual axiom that with increasing age will be increased consumption of prescription medicines.

Growing chronic diseases

The World Health Organization estimates that chronic diseases—such as cancer, heart disease, and respiratory and infectious diseases—account for approximately 43 million deaths annually, a figure that is likely to increase as a result of smoking, poor dietary habits, and sedentary lifestyles. Increasingly, pharmaceuticals are being used to control the adverse effects of these chronic diseases, enhance quality of life, and lengthen life spans. Cancer, CNS (central nervous system) conditions (e.g., depression, anxiety, psychosis), gastrointestinal and cardiovascular diseases are conditions where patients have greatly benefited from prescription medicines. The industry currently has over 800 medicines in development to treat diseases associated with aging (e.g., Alzheimer's disease, heart disease, diabetes, and cancer).

As we noted, people are taking more drugs for a variety of reasons. It is undeniable that extensive advertising of mass-marketed drugs is prompting people to request drugs from their physicians. With consumers generating demand, doctors are increasingly confronted with patients requesting specific drugs during a consultation, effectively turning the physician-patient relationship on its head. But other factors are at work here. Doctors are prescribing more prescription medicines as a first-line of defense against chronic conditions, since they are less expensive than hospitalization, physician services and rehabilitation. Newer drugs often have more attractive side effect profiles (e.g., drugs for psychoses). Drug treatments are now available for previously untreated conditions, such as Alzheimer's disease, sepsis (commonly known as blood poisoning), and HIV/AIDS. Chronic diseases, such as high blood cholesterol, hypertension, diabetes, depression, and asthma are now easily treated pharmacologically.

Causes of Death in the U.S. by Disease Type in 2002

Rank	Disease Type	Estimated Number of Deaths*
1	Heart Diseases	696,000
2	Malignant Neoplasms (Cancer)	559,000
3	Cerebrovascular Diseases	163,000
4	Chronic Lower Respiratory Diseases	126,000
5	Accidents	102,000
6	Diabetes mellitus	73,000
7	Influenza and pneumonia	66,000
8	Alzheimer's disease	59,000
9	Kidney diseases	41,000
10	Septicemia	34,000
	Total Deaths	**2,448,000**

Numbers are rounded to nearest thousand

Sources: *National Vital Statistics Report, National Center for Health Statistics and S&P Industry Surveys*

Apart from being good for the bottom line, the increased used of medicines will have important consequences for consumers. First, morbidity and mortality will be reduced. According to a study by the London-based Office of Health Economics, pharmaceuticals will account for 10 to 40 percent of future reductions in heart disease mortality; 15 to 40 percent in cerebro-vascular disease; 28 to 65 percent in breast cancer; and 3 to 26 percent in lung cancer. Second, medical costs will be reduced. According to estimates by the Cambridge, MA-based National Bureau of Economic Research, replacing older medicines with newer ones increases drug spending by an average of $18 but reduces other healthcare costs by $129, resulting in a net saving of $111. Finally, greater use of medicines will create an increased quality of life for consumers. Industry studies claim that newer medicines contribute to reduced hospitalizations and surgery, fewer adverse effects from medication, decreased complications of disease, and increased worker productivity. Current seniors and aging Baby Boomers will likely remain more independent longer and require expensive nursing care later in life than their parents' generation.

Visit Vault at **www.vault.com** for insider company profiles, expert advice, career message boards, expert resume reviews, the Vault Job Board and more.

VAULT CAREER LIBRARY   27

Strategic Alliances with Biotechs

With pharmaceutical R&D productivity in decline, i.e., more and more research dollars yielding fewer and fewer truly innovative new drugs, companies have also turned to strategic alliances with biotechs to add robustness to product pipelines. The contrast in the R&D status of the two industries could not be more stark.

The rate of growth in pharmaceutical R&D spending has been moderating in recent years, with total U.S. industry expenditures at $30 billion in 2001, $32 billion in 2002, and $33.2 billion in 2003. From another perspective, between 2000 and 2002, R&D spending as a percentage of sales remained relatively constant at 18.3%. In 2003, that percentage dipped to 17.7%. However you look at it, that hasn't been good news for the industry's main driver—innovation.

Over the same period, biotech funding has been rising steadily, despite the downturn in stock valuations in 2001. According to Burrill & Co., a merchant bank serving the life sciences industry and S&P Industry Surveys, biotech funding grew from $12 billion in 2001 to $10.4 billion in 2002 to $16.3 billion in 2003. Funding levels in 2004 should exceed those of 2003. Indeed, the biotech sector has been leading the way in innovation. In one study, the Boston Consulting Group (BCG) found that the 325 publicly traded biotechs accounted for only 3% of the drug industry's total R&D spending but are responsible for two-thirds of drugs in clinical trials. Most of these drugs fall in the "personalized medicine" category, i.e., they are destined for consumption by a relatively smaller patient population than the blockbusters Big Pharma currently markets.

Past success is one reason for the innovation gap. Conventional pharmaceuticals are based on only 500 validated biological targets. A target is a specific site on a cell for which researchers can design new medicines intended to have a highly specific effect on that site. Since the beginning of the industry in the 19th Century until the advent of genetics-based biotech products, the entire worldwide industry focused on those same 500 targets, creating more and more products, until virtually all targets had both new and imitative me-too products made for them. Targets have also been referred to as 'receptors.' The binding of a drug with its target site or receptor generates a reaction that has a positive intended effect, in lieu of destructive disease-progressing reaction.

New targets

But with the April 2003 announcement of the completion of the sequencing of the human genome by the International Human Genome Sequencing Consortium, researchers now have over 5,000 potential new targets for which to design new therapeutics and biologics. These new targets comprise a vast terrain on which the innovation engine can thrive. As of December 2003, the worldwide biotech market approached $37 billion, with the U.S. accounting for 62% of sales.

Because of this, Big Pharma executives have been steadily forging links with biotechs. According to Standard & Poor's, partnering deals between Big Pharma and Biotechs totaled $8.9 billion in 2003, up from $7.5 billion in 2002. Typically, these deals involve the In-licensing of products from R&D-based firms in return for cash and profit-sharing. This trend is expected to continue through the decade.

Examples of Recent (2003-2004) Alliances between Big Pharma and Biotechs

Big Pharma Company	Biotech	Type and Nature of Deal
Merck	H. Lundbeck A/S (Danish)	$270 million partnership for rights to an insomnia drug
Merck	Actelion, Ltd.	Venture to develop rennin inhibitors to treat hypertension and other cardio-renal diseases
Pfizer	Esperion Therapeutics	$1.3 billion acquisition (February 2004) for ETC-216, a potential blockbuster for HDL (high-density lipoprotein) therapy
Johnson & Johnson	Scios, Inc.	$2.4 billion acquisition
Johnson & Johnson	Millenium Pharmaceuticals	Reached agreement to co-promote Velcade, an anti-cancer drug outside the US

Sources: Standard & Poor's Industry Surveys

The combined R&D productivity picture is impressive. In 2003, the biopharmaceutical industry has been working on 402 anticancer drugs, 123 drugs to combat heart disease and stroke, 83 drugs and vaccines for HIV/AIDS, 176 drugs for neurological diseases, and 371 biotechnology products. That tallies to over 1,100 new products in the pipeline. Of those products, the number of expensive new biotech drugs is rapidly escalating. According to AdvancePCS, as of spring 2002, 75 biotech drugs had been approved for the marketplace and 370 such drugs were in development. Projections call for 800 products to be in clinical development by 2005. Biotech drugs continue to lead in treatments for cancer, autoimmune diseases, and inflammatory disorders. They will likely also help alleviate heart disease, eye disorders, genetic defects, infectious diseases, nephrology, and neurodegenerative conditions.

Innovative Therapeutics and Biologics in the Pipeline

Number of medicines	Treatment targets
371 biotech treatments . . .	Nearly half targeting cancer
395 medicines . . .	Targeting cancers of the lung, breast, colon, skin, prostate, and other cancers
123 medicines . . .	Targeting heart disease and stroke, including a vaccine to boost HDL, the "good" cholesterol
83 medicines and vaccines	Targeting HIV/AIDS, nine more than the 74 already approved
176 medicines and biologics	Targeting neurologic diseases, including 24 for Alzheimer's disease, 24 for brain tumors, 16 for multiple sclerosis, and 41 to alleviate pain

Sources: PhRMA Insights 2003

Patent Expirations

According to PhRMA, an estimated $100 billion of products will face patent expiration by 2005. Approximately $37 billion of that sum represents revenue loss from blockbuster drugs which face competition from less expensive generics. By 2006, nine mega-blockbusters will lose patent protection.

Effect of Loss of Patent Protection on Sales Volume of Blockbusters

Company	Drug	Sales Volume
Year Patent Protection Ended: 2002		
Astra Zeneca	Prilosec (antiulcer treatment)	$3.5 billion in 2001
Schering-Plough	Claritin (antihistamine)	$2.5 billion
Bristol-Myers Squibb	Glucophage (treatment for type II diabetes)	$2.0 billion
GlaxoSmithKline	Augmentin (antibiotic)	$1.8 billion
Year Patent Protection Ended: 2003		
GlaxoSmithKline	Wellbutrin XR (antidepressant)	$1.5 billion in 2002
Pfizer	Neurontin (anticonvulsant)	$1.4 billion
Aventis S.A.	Allegra (antihistamine)	$1.4 billion

Sources: Standard & Poor's Industry Surveys

This situation has created a challenging economic situation for industry executives. One popular tactic has been to extend the life of existing patents by reformulating drugs, adding indications, or combining drugs. While effective at protecting profits, critics have charged that such tactics are the industry's way of keeping already high prices high for longer periods of time. And pricing pressures are not likely to abet in the near future.

Drug Prices Expected to Rise

Industry leaders claim that they do not set prices. The marketplace sets prices. So, they charge as much as the unregulated U.S. market can bear. And really, it's not that prices are high, but rather, that medicines have less insurance coverage than other forms of healthcare, such as hospital stays and emergency room visits. Therefore, the solution to high-priced drugs is to expand coverage, which is expected in early 2006 (see below). According to health economist J.D. Kleinke, pharmaceuticals are "the cheapest weapon we have in our ongoing struggle against rising overall medical expenses." The industry also has made a concerted effort to estimate the value of its products to the healthcare economy. Rather than treat patients in advanced stages of disease or in emergency situations that might have been mitigated, PhRMA provides these examples of the value pharmaceuticals contribute to containing healthcare costs:

Visit Vault at **www.vault.com** for insider company profiles, expert advice, career message boards, expert resume reviews, the Vault Job Board and more.

VAULT CAREER LIBRARY   **31**

- Every dollar spent on medicines that lower diabetes patients' cholesterol produces $3 in health gains.

- Each additional dollar spent on new hormonal therapies to treat breast cancer results in at least $27 in health gains.

- Every dollar invested in beta-blockers to treat patients who have had heart attacks returns $38 in health gains.

- Every dollar spent on anti-platelet therapy for preventing stroke in high-risk patients has provided health gains valued at $2 to $6.

Many of these economic nuances are lost on consumers who are increasingly resisting high prices. Insurers and employers are also demanding healthcare cost containment. The industry has resisted the major tools used in Europe to reduce prices: government-negotiated price reductions, reference pricing, and utilization of less expensive generics.

Cost containment legislation of various kinds has been crafted on both the state and federal level. In May 2003, the Supreme Court ruling known as "Maine Rx" effectively forced drug manufacturers to lower state drug costs by extending Medicaid-mandated discounts to state residents without prescription drug coverage. Companies that refused or resisted compliance would be restricted from participating in Maine's Medicaid program and physicians will have to get authorization before prescribing those companies's products for Medicaid recipients. The Maine ruling serves as a model for other states to implement their own cost-containment programs.

And in December 2003, Congress passed the Medicare Prescription Drug, Improvement, and Modernization Act of 2003. This landmark legislation expands access and improves healthcare for some 41 million senior citizens. Starting in 2006, seniors will be able to sign up for a voluntary prescription drug benefit that will help defray out-of-pocket drug costs. The bill is based on letting private insurers compete to sign up subscribers, negotiate discounts for a large consumer base, provides for more screenings to detect health problems earlier, and enacts further efficiencies in approving generic drugs.

Continued Industry Consolidation

Big Pharma is a top-heavy industry. The top 10 companies accounted for about 50% of global pharmaceutical sales in 2003, according to IMS Health, Inc., a pharmaceutical market research firm. In 1990, the top ten garnered only 28% of global sales. This increased concentration has permitted companies to create operational efficiencies, round out product offerings, and exit non-core businesses (such as animal health products and consumer products).

In recent years, two already large players merged. With its $90 billion acquisition of Warner-Lambert in 2000 and $58 billion Pharmacia in 2003, Pfizer is now the world's largest pharmaceutical company and a virtual proxy for understanding the industry. According to Standard and Poor's Industry Analysis, potential merger candidates include Bristol-Myers Squibb, Wyeth, and Schering-Plough.

Recent Pharmaceutical Industry Consolidations: 1995—2003

Merging Entity	Merging Entity	New Company
Glaxo-Wellcome (UK)	Smith-Kline Beecham (US)	GlaxoSmithKline PLC (UK)
Pfizer (US)	Warner-Lambert (US)	Pfizer (US)
Pfizer (US)	Pharmacia (US)	Pfizer (US)
Pharmacia (Sweden)	Upjohn (US)	Pharmacia & Upjohn (US)
Astra (Sweden)	Zeneca (UK)	AstraZeneca PLC (UK)
Hoechst Marion Roussel (Germany)	Rhone-Poulenc Rorer (France)	Aventis (France)

Sources: Standard & Poor's Industry Surveys

Spending on Direct-to-Consumer Advertising

It's hard to spend more than a couple of hours watching television without running across commercials urging us to question our doctors about one of the industry's products. You should expect more directo-to-consumer (DTC) advertising in the coming years. Growth rates since 1997, when the industry obtained approval to advertise on TV, are impressive. In 2003, the industry spent $3.3 billion in print and airwave (radio and TV) ads, up from $1 billion in 1997—a 230% increase. Indeed, drugs have become the tenth-largest category of advertised products in the U.S.

The so-called "lifestyle" drugs are typically the most heavily targeted for DTC advertising, i.e., those for chronic conditions whose consumption can be curtailed as prices increase. The idea is that when the price goes up, people will consume less. Examples include antidepressants (e.g., Paxil and Prozak), heartburn medicines (e.g., Nexium), and erectile dysfunction drugs (e.g., Viagra or Cialis). The mass promotion of these drugs has likely extended to consumers who can do without some of these medicines occasionally. On the other hand, there are subsets of these patient groups, such as those with a genuine propensity to fall into clinical depression, for whom antidepressants are an essential part of a productive life. Cholesterol-lowering drugs, a 'necessary' drug for many patients, is one of the most aggressively advertised product categories. In 2004, the product most heavily promoted was Pfizer's Lipitor, with $712 million in sales, up 33% over 2003.

In May 2004, The FTC (Federal Trade Commission) announced new guidelines that built on the FDA guidelines published in February 2004. They required advertisers to state a drug's risks more explicitly (in bullet lists instead of tiny print) for print advertisements. In late 2004, the FDA ordered Pfizer to pull its "Wild Thing" Viagra ads because they failed to disclose what condition Viagra treats and what the drug's major side effects are.

Critics have attacked the industry as pushing expensive, over-priced medicines on the public and on attempting to expand its consumer base by encouraging people to seek prescription drugs from their physicians. That has certainly struck a cord and industry leaders (notably Pfizer CEO Henry A. McKinnell) publicly acknowledged that, although DTC advertising will continue, it should be more focused on target patient populations and more forthright on the actual effects of their products on consumers.

Industry's Global Outlook is Positive

The international industry is primarily located in Great Britain, the European Union, and Japan, all of whom have tightly regulated pharmaceutical industries with strict price controls and similar efforts at cost containment as in the U.S. market. With downward pressure on profits, the European companies, once thought of as innovation leaders, lost their edge to their U.S. counterparts in the 1990s. Indeed, since the turn of the millennium, European companies have actually increased their investments in U.S. And according to Standard & Poor's, the global industry can expect moderate sales growth over the next few years.

The expanded European Union (EU) is likely to have a double-edged effect on the pharmaceutical industry. Fifteen new nations were admitted on May 1, 2004 to create the current 25-member union. On the positive side, EU expansion means that new member nations will have to accept the intellectual property rights adopted by older members. This will spur innovation by creating an incentive to risk capital to develop new products. And that, in turn, will be good for the industry, the consumer, and the overall regional market (via employment and economic development). On the negative side, more sources of cheaper drugs will become available. This happens through the arbitrage-like transactions referred to earlier as "parallel trade." Standard & Poor's estimated that parallel trade in pharmaceuticals amounted to over $12 billion in 2003.

Visit Vault at **www.vault.com** for insider company profiles, expert advice, career message boards, expert resume reviews, the Vault Job Board and more.

VAULT CAREER LIBRARY   35

Major Issues and Challenges

CHAPTER 3

Reimportation or Sourcing of Drugs

Buying cheaper drugs from Canadian pharmacies is a hot topic today. The practice is called "reimportation," a term that has been widely used in the media and refers to the process of a pharmaceutical company selling American-manufactured and FDA-approved drugs at discounts to Canadian pharmacies, which consumers seeking cheaper prices then reimport back into the U.S. If this sounds a bit confusing at first, here's the sequence of transactions. A pharmaceutical company sells its products to a Canadian pharmacy at government-controlled discounted prices. Consumers in the U.S. know this. They go to the pharmacy's Web site (or contact the pharmacy by phone), then order the same drug at that sale price instead of going to a local U.S. pharmacy to fill their prescription and pay U.S. prices. The Canadian pharmacy gets the business and the consumer a price break.

The industry is fighting strenuously against this practice, citing the danger to public health stemming from lack of safeguards against shoddy overseas manufacturing from unknown sources. Even President Bush commented on this possibility in one of the 2004 Presidential debates. But whatever drug executives and the politicians who support them say about the public's safety being their main concern, many Americans are fast learning that it is the industry's pricing structure that is being threatened.

The reality is that foreign consumers—Canadians, Europeans, Japanese—typically pay from 25% to 50% less for prescription drugs than Americans for the same product. This is because their governments negotiate prices with drug companies. With large consumer bases, public health officials can negotiate steep discounts for large volumes of prescription medicines. In the U.S., no such mechanism is in place for the largest consumer base—the elderly on Medicare.

Consumers and MCOs

Reimportation happens through several channels. Over 100 Canadian Internet-based pharmacies serve consumer needs. Many consumers in states across from the border take bus trips to Canada to purchase their medicines. Exactly how consumers find out about those sites is anybody's guess. But consumers determined to save a buck are most resourceful. A few tech-savvy consumers who find sites may broadcast their findings in chat rooms and online bulletin boards, thus spreading the word. According to IMS Health, in 2003, reimported Canadian drugs totaled about $675 million, up from $414 million in 2002, and represented a 63% increase. The dollar volume is likely to continue to increase despite industry opposition.

Strictly speaking, though importing drugs from foreign countries is illegal, both the government and the industry have not prosecuted the large number of mostly senior citizens from seeking relief from high prices. Now, however, even managed care organizations (MCOs) are looking into reimporting drugs as a cost-containment measure. Should MCOs succeed in reimporting drugs, the pressure on the industry will be even greater. This is because individuals purchase drugs for themselves alone, whereas MCOs bulk-purchase millions of units of medicines, making the drag on profits much more significant. But a trend is hard to beat. With the American Association of Retired Persons (AARP) weighing in in favor of reimportation, as well as many Republican politicians, reimportation policy is sure to get a second look in the next few years.

Pricing

Pricing is one of the most significant and controversial aspects of pharmaceutical marketing. Traditionally, changes in macroeconomic conditions have not affected pharmaceutical markets, largely because demand for medicines was based on the population's health. With limited alternate therapies for many diseases and reimbursement of the bulk of drug costs by third-party insurance payers, demand for many pharmaceutical products has been relatively impervious to price changes.

What has been changing in recent years, however, is the trend to shifting a greater proportion of healthcare dollars from employers and insurers to consumers. Many plans have limited or no prescription drug coverage. In addition, until the Medicare Prescription Drug Benefit goes into effect in 2006, most elderly had to pay out-of-pocket for their prescription drugs. With the public increasingly aware of the price differential between American and overseas markets, the clamor for price containment will likely continue.

The industry has steadfastly maintained that prices reflect the need to recoup R&D investment and that only three in ten drugs recoup their development costs. This means that that burden plus creating profits also falls on those few drugs. Hence, the need for pricing meets these objectives. What the industry says is true, but it is not the whole story. In addition to development costs, several other factors contribute to pricing strategy, including the relative efficacy of a given drug versus its rivals, the size of the target market(s), the price of competing therapeutics, and whether a drug is a breakthrough therapy, in which case it will be priced substantially above others in its class.

The industry knows that prices of newly launched drugs are set high. Indeed, one segment of the sales training programs for pharmaceutical sales representatives focuses on how to overcome physician objections to high prices. Reps do call on both physicians and pharmacists, but the latter often work for big chains, who agree to stock drugs via bulk orders. Justification for premium prices includes better tolerance profiles, more convenient delivery systems, and fewer interactions with other prescribed drugs. Although physicians themselves do not pay for the drugs, many are sensitive to patients' economic concerns and will recommend a less expensive drug if it works just as well as a branded drug. Faced with increasing price resistance, the industry has emphasized that drug companies have very few years in which to recoup development costs before patents protection expires. With development timetables consuming 12 to 15 years of the 20-year patent protection period, pharmaceutical marketers have only a few years in which to recoup those gargantuan costs. This is yet another challenge facing the industry.

Generics

The sale of generics poses a continuing challenge for the industry. A "generic" is a product whose original patent has expired and which can now be produced and supplied by companies other than the one which held the original patent. Generic products are also known as multi-source drugs or products. After a drug's patent protection ends, the price of its generic form is usually about 60% that of the branded drug. Several generic versions may become available after a year or two, by which time the average price of a generic may drop to 20% that of its branded counterpart.

The U.S. has the largest generics market of the three major drug markets—the U.S., Europe and Japan. And by all indications, the generics business is booming. IMS Health estimates that generics accounted for 54% of all prescriptions in the U.S. in 2003. This figure includes the so-called "branded generics," drugs whose patents have expired but which have been reformulated to achieve more convenient dosage regimen (e.g., one-a-day pill with controlled release vs. two or three pills per day). The generics category also includes regular generics (i.e., branded pharmaceuticals sold under their trade names). Sales of generic drugs grew by over 20% in 2004, with double-digit growth in sight for most of this decade, and the U.S. market is estimated to reach $21.6 billion by 2005. Factors contributing to this growth include the ending of patent protection for some $35 billion in branded pharmaceuticals, and unrelenting pricing pressure from both managed care and government to contain costs, partly by using less expensive generics. These factors have already made an impact on the branded industry. The proportion of generics' share in the U.S. overall prescription drug market has been growing steadily in this decade, with PhRMA estimating that it will reach 57% by 2005. The leading generics companies in the U.S. are Faulding and Teva; each company has annual sales of over $1.2 billion.

A major milestone in the U.S. generics industry is the Waxman-Hatch Act, which makes it possible for generics manufacturers to prepare to launch their product even before the patent on the original brand has expired. This legislation hits right at the bottom line, since the generic version can be made ready to hit the market essentially the day after the patent on its branded counterpart has expired. Consequently, the generics manufacturer loses no time—and hence no sales revenue—on development after a branded drug's patent protection period has ended. The other big implication has been for consumers. The Congressional Budget Office has estimated that generic drugs save U.S. consumers $8 to $10 billion annually.

Direct-to-Consumer (DTC) Advertising

Direct-to-consumer advertising is likely to continue to grow in the American market. In 2003, the industry spent some $3.3 billion. That figure is expected to grow to $7.2 billion by 2007, a valid expectation since the industry knows that DTC advertising works, i.e., it helps sell prescription drugs. According to one study, as a result of DTC ads, some 20% of consumers were prompted to call their physicians to inquire about a drug.

Retailer Henry Wanamaker: *". . . half of my advertising is wasted; the trouble is I don't know which half."*

In recent years, the industry's aggressive promotion to consumers has drawn criticism from watchdog groups, consumer advocacy groups and others, who claimed that direct promotion to consumers undercut the physician's role as decision-maker. Patients can demand a specific drug from their physicians, instead of what the doctor feels is most appropriate, the argument went. This argument gained currency with physician reports that patients came into consultations with specific notions of how they should be treated. The industry pointed out that the simple fact that patients suggest a medicine to a physician does not necessarily guarantee a prescription will be written: the physician retains the right to either not prescribe anything or, alternatively, prescribe something else. That may be the case, but the sheer density of DTC ads on television has changed the doctor-patient dynamic.

Another criticism is that DTC ads are a clever market-expansion strategy, with people going in to see doctors to get prescriptions for conditions that may be treatable through either natural or over-the-counter (OTC) products, both of which are often less expensive than prescription medicines. Third, some industry critics believe that Americans are way overmedicated, turning to drugs instead of relieving stresses naturally and changing bad lifestyle habits.

In justifying its use of DTC to promote its products, PhRMA publications make several points. First, DTC ads help educate patients about new treatment options and encourage greater dialogue between patients and their physicians about all available options. Second, DTC ads lead patients to contact physicians about illnesses earlier than they otherwise would have. Third, previously undiagnosed conditions are identified when a patient seeks out a physician for a condition he may think he has as a result of observing DTC ads. For example, a man who goes to see a doctor for erectile dysfunction after seeing a Viagra ad may discover other conditions such as hypertension or heart disease. Fourth, once prescribed, compliance to drug regimens is higher. The industry's bottom line attitude is that DTC advertising effectively strengthens the doctor-patient relationship and serves an important role in maintaining good health.

R&D vs. Promotion Expenditures in 2002 ($ billion)

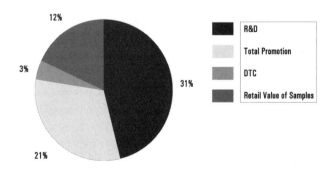

Sources: Standard & Poor's Industry Surveys

Visit Vault at **www.vault.com** for insider company profiles, expert advice, career message boards, expert resume reviews, the Vault Job Board and more.

VAULT CAREER LIBRARY   **41**

The fact is that both sides of this debate have valid points. As a potential pharmaceutical marketer, choosing a career in the fields related to producing DTC ads will likely pose a continuing challenge. In 2004, expanded FDA regulations tightened rules overseeing the content of DTC ads, requiring a greater emphasis on highlighting the risks associated with the advertised drug and patient groups who should not take the drug. In 2005, DTC ads were more subdued. Promotion of the brand itself played a subordinate part to the drug's main and adverse effects, with clear description of risks to specific groups.

Ethics in Marketing Pharmaceuticals

On July 1, 2002, the industry adopted a new, voluntary ethical code on marketing its products to healthcare professionals. The New Code on Interactions with Healthcare Professionals provides guidelines to pharmaceutical sales representatives and other marketing professionals on how to handle everything from entertainment freebies, to the distribution of free samples and coordination of physician education meetings. The Code extends only to industry marketers and places no restrictions on physicians. The Code emerged from growing criticism that the plethora of giveaways to physicians erodes their objectivity in writing prescriptions. Despite howls of protest, the industry was able to put this Code into effect, and with the trade association PhRMA's endorsement, all member companies become required to adhere to it in order to maintain membership in good standing.

Briefly, the Code stipulates that interactions should be "focused on informing healthcare professionals about products, providing scientific and educational information, and supporting medical research and education," according to PhRMA President Alan F. Holmer. The Code severely restricts offers of entertainment to include only activities that promote the transfer of scientific and medical information. Previously, physicians were courted with offers of tickets to sporting events, special meals, and the like. Even the support of an industry staple, conferences and symposia, where academic and industry researchers exchange ideas, came under scrutiny. Companies are now recommended to support only conference sponsors, rather than individual participants. Specifically, this means providing support to an academic group (e.g., American Association of Oncologists) to help defray the expenses of putting on a symposium rather than covering the travel expenses of individual oncologists who would be presenting papers at the meeting. Consulting fees are now to be restricted solely to payment for a physician's expertise, and not as a reward or inducement to prescribe a specific medication. Finally, most companies offer a plethora of items to physicians to educate their patients and maintain their practices. Everything from information sheets on specific conditions to notepads to mugs are routinely given to physicians in order to keep a drug company and its product name in front of them. The new Code restricts such freebies to $100 or less.

Although voluntary, the new guidelines have been widely adopted. But in early 2005, consulting continues to be controversial, with critics pointing out that physicians accepting consulting fees effectively have a conflict of interest. Since the Vioxx recall, this provision in the Code is likely to come under increasing scrutiny. The industry understands that self-regulation is better than government regulation, and hopes the steps it has taken will alleviate public concerns. The debate over drug safety evaluation in the next few years should help the industry determine if its guidelines go far enough.

Drug Safety Evaluation and Approval at the FDA

The Vioxx recall and restriction of advertising on other Cox-2 inhibitors (Celebrex and Bextra) in its aftermath challenged the American public's trust in the regulatory process and the FDA. Millions of people were affected and potentially tens of thousands of heart attacks occurred because of this class of painkillers. The Merck CEO, Ray Gilmartin, became the face of the industry in September 2004. A few months later, Pfizer CEO Henry McKinnell also hit the airwaves to explain his company's position on keeping Celebrex in the market but withdrawing its television ads. For several months, reporters, analysts, and Congress probed and explored the problem. A whistleblower from inside the FDA, Dr. David Graham, sharply criticized the agency for its current practices around drug safety and approval.

In early 2005, three core problems needed to be worked out between the industry and its government regulators. How are long-term, broad-based clinical trials to be financed and implemented? The so-called Phase III trials are meant to determine whether a drug is both safe and effective in large patient populations, but identifying patients for the clinical trials and following their progress over years is prohibitively costly and eats into the patent protection period. With expedited approvals, companies get their products to market, then follow the incidence of adverse effects on the large-scale patient groups to whom the products are mass-marketed. This practice effectively makes consumers the final set of guinea pigs. Second, the recall made the public aware of the fundamental change in the relationship between

Visit Vault at **www.vault.com** for insider company profiles, expert advice, career message boards, expert resume reviews, the Vault Job Board and more.

VAULT CAREER LIBRARY   **43**

the FDA and the industry that occurred in the mid-1990s, when the industry was asked to pay fees to the FDA to defray the costs of testing. Some critics hold that a fully independent body should conduct clinical trials, while others feel this action would create needless complexity to an already complex process. The third problem is how companies can accurately communicate clinical trial results, including the adverse effects of a drug, to consumers and watchdog groups.

The industry has already responded, with some companies posting clinical trial results on their Web sites to show that they are not holding back information from the public. This is a constructive step, but further negotiation, compromise, and reform are expected in order to retrieve the public's trust.

Issues in the Global Pharmaceutical Industry

Over one-third of the industry's sales are generated in overseas markets, with the highest concentrations coming from the United Kingdom, the European Union and Japan. Other geographies, notably India, China, and Latin America, are considered emerging markets. With this growing global span come several ongoing challenges, such as regulatory differences, cost-containment regimes, and patent protection.

Even though the pricing of drugs is not subject to government controls, virtually every phase of drug development beyond initial discovery in the U.S. is regulated. The three-stage clinical trial testing and subsequent fourth post-market introduction phase is subject to FDA scrutiny. The call for even tighter safety standards in the current environment is increasing. Yet the clinical trial process and the voluminous documentation required at every step of the multi-phase process is not as stringent in foreign countries, making it difficult to obtain the full details of safety and clinical trial results. This lack of transparency in regulatory practices makes it hard to know which country's new medicines should be approved for marketing in the U.S. Finally, just making sense of the different regulations across national and regional markets poses yet another challenge.

Containing costs

All other established markets have heavy involvement of their governments in containing costs, accomplished via aggressive price discounts. While good for consumers in the short run, this practice has had unfortunate consequences. First, discounting prices reduces profits, which in turn reduces earnings available for R&D. In the 1990s, the European pharmaceutical industry, long the center of global innovation, lost its place to the U.S., as thinning margins eroded R&D investment. The U.S. gained and has maintained its edge in innovation. Now the U.S. industry is under pressure to contain its share of healthcare costs. With government-mandated price reductions in major markets, the American consumer has been left carrying the burden of funding R&D. The challenge is how to obtain agreement from major overseas market regulators to fund their fair share of R&D for the benefit of all. In America, the industry sets prices at what the market will bear, knowing that it can achieve its profit goals in this unregulated marketplace, which has left the industry vulnerable to all kinds of bad press. The debate would change if included in the discussion was a strategy to get the Europeans and Japanese to pay for innovation.

Cost-containment regimes also discriminate against newer, innovative products, which are usually more expensive than established medicines. That may not sound particularly consequential, but consider a cancer patient undergoing chemotherapy. The side effects include nausea, vomiting, and constipation, among others. Ten or 15 years ago, cancer patients required hospitalization since the side effects were so severe. Today, newer medications to manage these same side effects enable such patients to undergo chemotherapy treatments on an outpatient basis. This is not only more cost-effective, but it also enhances the quality of life for patients.

Counterfeits

There is no question that protecting patents is easier in more established markets, since those markets develop and market their own products, and hence, have an interest in protecting their own intellectual property. Emerging markets, notably China, constitute a wild frontier in enforcing intellectual property rights. China is especially notorious for permitting widespread violations of copyrights and patents on all manner of goods— from music videos and CDs to auto parts and electronic goods. Recently, China was reported to account for nearly two-thirds of counterfeit goods. In the pharmaceutical industry, Pakistan and Russia are leading producers of fake drugs. In fact, the World Health Organization estimates that about 10% of medicines worldwide are counterfeit, representing a loss of some $46 billion in revenues annually to the industry.

Visit Vault at **www.vault.com** for insider company profiles, expert advice, career message boards, expert resume reviews, the Vault Job Board and more.

VAULT CAREER LIBRARY   **45**

But monetary loss is not the only problem with fake drugs. Patient safety is at risk from the cheap, and sometimes toxic, ingredients used to simulate the appearance of real drugs. In 2003, a phone call from a consumer complaining that a tablet of the cholesterol-lowering drug, Lipitor, tasted bitter led to testing that confirmed it was fake. That, in turn led to the removal of some 16.5 million tablets from pharmacies. Later in 2003, law enforcement in Asia discovered 1.5 million counterfeit doses of Pfizer's hypertension drug, Novarsc. Fake doses of Viagra have also surfaced. Novartis discovered that counterfeiters had used yellow highway paint to simulate the color of one of its painkillers. One report had up to 40% of medicines in Africa as counterfeit, creating another layer of risk to populations battling HIV/AIDS.

The industry has fought back on multiple fronts, but concedes that this is a long-term problem. Pfizer is using technology to tag its products: later in 2005, it will place radio-frequency ID tags on Viagra sold in the U.S. Another tactic is to lobby the federal government to bring a complaint to the World Trade Organization. Recently, U.S. diplomats have voiced their displeasure over Chinese trade policy directly to the Chinese leadership. Interestingly, the U.S., European Union, and Japan are bringing a united front against counterfeiting, something the Chinese government has noticed. Although it has written new laws, the Chinese government has generally turned a blind eye to widespread theft of intellectual property, except where it involves two domestic companies and harms individual Chinese citizens. Since the Chinese are investing heavily in biopharmaceutical research, protecting their own homegrown discoveries should prove to be an effective motivator, now that their own interests are at stake. Until that happens, however, inadequate protection of intellectual property will effectively eliminate access to that market, reduce incentives to search for cures, continue to drag companies down economically, and potentially harm unwitting consumers.

Bioterrorism and Other Public Health Issues

Bioterrorism

The terrorist attacks of September 11, 2001 made the need for an anti-bioterror policy apparent. The biopharmaceutical industry is particularly affected by this new threat, since it is the source of vaccines for the leading bioterror threats, among which are anthrax, smallpox, plague, and other germ-based diseases. The industry has responded to this challenge from multiple perspectives simultaneously.

Last year, Congress passed the Project Bioshield Act of 2004, a comprehensive effort involving several federal agencies to protect Americans against chemical, biological, radiological, or nuclear (CBRN) attack. Among other things, the provision permits the FDA to expedite availability of promising treatments in the event of an attack, allows for the purchase and stockpiling of large-scale quantities of drugs and vaccines, and advances research into the next generation of treatments against CBRN substances. For its part, the industry has acknowledged the reasonableness of these measures yet continues to lobby for improved protection against product liability for those products designed to be used against bioterror threats.

Knowing that security breaches in its work against bioterror threats can undermine not only the economic status of its research, but also the national security, in June 2004, 12 major biopharmaceutical companies came together to form the SAFE Initiative. "Secure Access for Everyone" or SAFE established an industry standard for the global digital identity of scientific and clinical documentation, essential for the electronic transfer of the thousands of pages of regulatory submissions, large databases gathered in clinical trials and massive genomic data sets generated in discovery research. SAFE reduces identity management costs, secures e-business transactions, and facilitates e-submissions to regulators. What all of this means is that knowledge and information on anti-bioterror vaccines and drugs in development can be transferred from scientists and clinicians to government regulators without falling into the hands of terrorists.

Vaccines

The 2004 shortage of flu vaccine made public the need to secure the nation's vaccine supply, for both flu and other diseases. The fundamental problem is one of sourcing and economics. With low profit-margins and high product liability, vaccines are not deemed to be economically viable ventures by many drug manufacturers. The liability is incurred if a vaccine fails to protect a patient, who in turn holds the vaccine manufacturer responsible for his illness. When one of a few sources encounters a problem, as with the flu vaccine, a huge gap in supply is created.

One partial potential solution involves improving the manufacturing method with newer cell culture techniques. This advancement will ensure speedier manufacturing methods that will, in turn, make more supply available faster.

Visit Vault at **www.vault.com** for insider company profiles, expert advice, career message boards, expert resume reviews, the Vault Job Board and more.

VAULT CAREER LIBRARY   47

Another solution is to increase the price of the vaccine, so that manufacturers can achieve a marginal return that is enough above their marginal costs to encourage more producers to enter the market. The price for vaccines is determined by the government, which has an interest in keeping prices as low as possible. Were the price set by the marketplace, as in conventional drugs, the situation would likely be ameliorated, as consumers would determine that it is in their interest to have a vaccine and would then be willing to pay for it. More producers would then find it attractive to enter the market, but would have to compete with each other to determine the price the market will bear.

Leaving the market to set the price makes vaccines inaccessible to the poor, and changes in manufacturing methods take time. The flu vaccine shortage (due to a shutdown at Chiron, one of only two manufacturers, as described earlier) embarrassed the government, and created anxiety in citizens and ridicule among industry critics. In early 2005, massive outbreaks of the flu have not materialized. In late 2005, scares of an avian flu pandemic have changed the debate. As noted earlier, government and industry executives are collaborating to expand production and stockpile inventories of Tamiflu (the best agent currently known to fight avian flu symptoms) and other flu vaccines in anticipation of the 2005-6 flu season.

Discovery, Testing & Approval Process

CHAPTER 4

The Drug Discovery, Testing, and Approval Process

The process of bringing a drug to market is the same for both conventional and biotech drugs, since both classes are submitted to animal testing, limited clinical trials, and large-scale extended-term clinical trials. This is often a period of 10-15 years. Many people spend their entire careers focused on one phase of the process, such as discovery research. Others become specialists in a single functional area, such as clinical research or business development.

Diagnostic testing devices or other types of medical devices generally go through a less rigorous approval process to get to market since humans do not ingest these products. Hence, the complex and expensive clinical trials are unnecessary and FDA approval times are generally shorter.

An Overview of the Process

The drug discovery, testing, and approval process in the U.S. is the most rigorous in the world, often taking years and hundreds of millions of dollars. The central goal is to provide the public with medications that are both safe and effective. The major steps in the process are the same, as we pointed out, for regular and biopharmaceuticals, and are listed below followed by the average number of months required to obtain FDA approval (approximately 24 months). It's important to understand this process because it provides the framework around which all biopharmaceutical products are shepherded from the laboratory ultimately to the marketplace.

- Discovery
- Preclinical testing
- Phase I
- Phase II
- Phase III
- FDA Review and Approval
- Post-marketing Testing

The following diagram illustrates the drug development process for both regular and biopharmaceuticals.

Drug Development Stages

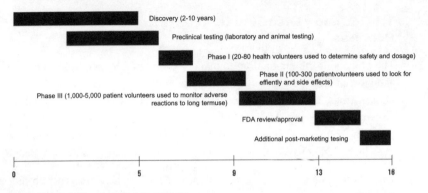

Sources: *Pharmaceutical Research and Manufacturers of America.*

Sources: Standard & Poor's Industry Surveys

Until the Vioxx recall, the FDA was praised for streamlining the FDA review process, as shown below. In the months following the September 2004 voluntary recall by Merck, industry observers wondered whether this outcome is truly in the best interests of American consumers. The industry had lobbied to get its products to market well within the patent protection period (currently 20 years) so that it could recoup its investment. Presently the drug development and approval process eats into at least half that period, leaving at most 10 years of patent protection. In the current climate of reflection and reform, the trendline for FDA review times is likely to change.

FDA Review Times

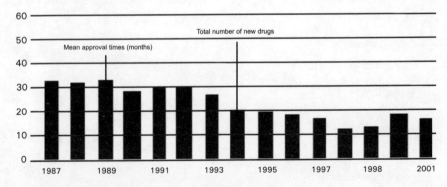

Sources: Pharmaceutical Research and Manufacturers of America

Discovery

The pharmaceutical industry invests billions of dollars each year on R&D (some $33.2 billion in 2003 alone). The initial phase of R&D, called the discovery phase, can be broken down into several steps. Understanding how discovery research proceeds will provide you with a broader perspective, especially if you are considering a career in the laboratory.

Step	Description
Identify Target	Focus is on identifying genes and their respective products, which are suspected to cause a specific disease. **Goal:** Find and isolate potential areas for therapeutic intervention.
Validate Target	Once the target has been identified, its role in the disease must then be understood. Techniques such as differential gene expression, tissue distribution analysis, and protein pathway studies help verify a genetic target's role in disease formation. **Goal:** Understand the target's role in disease
Develop Assay	A drug candidate screening process or "assay" is then developed to detect the activity that potential drug treatments have on the target molecule. An assay is a procedure that tests the drug by measuring a key biochemical parameter. An ideal assay is cost-effective, fast, accurate, easy to perform, quantitative, and amenable to automation. **Goal:** Find a way to test a potential drug's effect on the target
Conduct Primary Screening	Compounds are then identified that have a minimum level of effect or activity against the target molecule. Drug developers then include these "hits" in subsequent screens. Since it is not known exactly which drug structure will be most effective, scientists test hundreds of variations to find the one with optimal biological activity. A common technique is high-throughput screening, in which hundreds of molecules are tested simultaneously and the data output collected on computers. **Goal:** Find active drug candidates or "hits"

Visit Vault at **www.vault.com** for insider company profiles, expert advice, career message boards, expert resume reviews, the Vault Job Board and more.

V/\ULT CAREER LIBRARY   **51**

Step	Description
Conduct Secondary Screening	Results from the primary screen are confirmed. In addition to its activity, the candidate drug's potency and selectivity are also determined. Drug developers thus identify the candidate drug molecule with the most promising pharmacologic profile. Secondary screening is often done manually, with each active molecule tested separately, and is thus more costly than primary. **Goal:** Find the most promising drug candidates
Optimize Leads	Once the most promising candidates have been identified, yet another screening step is made to identify the most promising candidate relative to safety and therapeutic efficacy. The products of these screens are incorporated in new libraries of compounds. This step can incorporate 10 or more iterations over previously screened groups. **Goal:** Identify the drug candidates or "leads" with the best safety and therapeutic efficacy profiles.

Preclinical testing

Step	Description
Preclinical studies	Leads are then submitted to a set of FDA-mandated animal tests before clinical trials on humans can begin. Animal testing is used to assess a lead's potential carcinogenicity and other toxicity. Other pharmacologic properties of the compound are also tested. The results of testing in this phase are incorporated in an Investigational New Drug Application (INDA), which is submitted to the FDA before human clinical testing commences. **Goal:** Assess the drug's toxicity in animals

Clinical Testing

The results of this rigorous process are sobering.

For each 20 drugs entering clinical testing:

- On average, 13 to 14 complete Phase I.

- Of those, 9 complete Phase II.

- One or two survive Phase III.

This means that only 5-10% of candidate drugs submitted for clinical trials are approved for marketing, making the U.S. drug approval process the most restrictive in the world, and relatively low compared to approval rates in other developed countries. However, there has been a move to rationalize drug approval within large blocks, such as the EU, to create a single standard among all member states, as opposed to older standards, where each country approved medicines developed within its own borders. Nevertheless, a drug approved anywhere in the world must still be approved by the FDA before it can be marketed in the U.S.

Step	Description
Phase I	The candidate drug is administered in small doses initially to a relatively small number of healthy people to test its safety. If proven successful, the dosage is slowly increased to determine the candidate drug's safety at higher levels. **Goal:** Test the safety of the drug
Phase II	The candidate drug is then administered to patients suffering from the disease the drug is intended to treat. Phase II tests seek to evaluate the drug's effectiveness and safety, includes a larger population of subjects and a longer test period than Phase I. **Goal:** Test the efficacy of the drug

Visit Vault at www.vault.com for insider company profiles, expert advice, career message boards, expert resume reviews, the Vault Job Board and more.

VAULT CAREER LIBRARY   53

Step	Description
Phase III	Testing here is the most complex and rigorous and often involves even larger groups of ill patients, who are monitored closely to determine the candidate drug's efficacy and identify adverse reactions. Tests are double-blind (neither doctor nor patient knows whether the drug administered is the real test drug or a placebo, a harmless comparison pill with no biological effect). In order to further remove the possibility of bias, the distribution of test drugs and placebos is randomized, so that the clinical physician cannot guess whether he is using the test drug or placebo on any given test patient. **Goal:** Verify the drug's safety, effectiveness, and optimum dosage regimens

FDA Review and Approval

Step	Description
Filing of Biologics License Application (BLA) or New Drug Application (NDA)	The BLA and NDA are summaries of all aspects of a candidate drug's profile and intended use. They are compiled by the manufacturer and submitted to the FDA. BLAs and NDAs contain complete details on the molecular structure and formulation, the results of all phases of testing, production methods, labeling content, and intended patient use. BLAs and NDAs sometimes exceed 100,000 pages of text. Typically, the FDA requires 18 months to approve a drug after the manufacturer submits these documents.

Post-marketing testing

Step	Description
Additional indications	After introduction into the marketplace, the manufacturer often submits supplemental NDAs to obtain approval of a drug for other additional indications.
Post-launch monitoring	The FDA continues to monitor a drug after it enters the marketplace. If side effects show up when a drug is in wide use, the FDA may request an additional phase (Phase IV) of testing to determine the long-term effects of a drug. This duration of this phase varies and can last many years, depending on whether the FDA feels ongoing monitoring on market-size populations is warranted.
Regulatory measures	The FDA may order a product recall if either the safety or efficacy of a drug is questioned. This can happen under several circumstances, including defective packaging, misleading labeling, failure to meet disintegration or content uniformity tests, loss of sterility, subpotency, or lack of evidence of effectiveness.

The debate over drug safety evaluation centers on Phases III and IV of the approval process. The Phase system was developed to determine the safety of a drug first in animals. Only then was a drug's efficacy tested on human subjects. By Phase III, datasets collected on large patient populations ideally identify the usually small (in percentage terms) subset that will experience adverse effects, such as the cardiac problems in a group of patients taking Vioxx over a long period of time. Any dangers to the public are supposed to be identified prior to market launch. Follow-up Phase IV studies provide additional data on long-term effects in mega-population sets (in the millions, rather than the thousands, as in Phase III).

Should the FDA push back and demand that Phase III testing be expanded beyond its current scope to identify at-risk subsets of consumer groups prior to launch? The industry claims that clinical trials can become so extended that they delay the introduction of products and thus extend needless suffering as well as compromise the industry financially. The argument is that only in post-marketing monitoring can statistically tiny groups of patients (thousands in a consumer cohort of millions) become identified. At the end of 2005, the court hearing the Merck Vioxx case put the onus on the

Visit Vault at **www.vault.com** for insider company profiles, expert advice, career message boards, expert resume reviews, the Vault Job Board and more.

VAULT CAREER LIBRARY   55

manufacturer to demonstrate its product's safety. The final chapter will be written in the years to come, but the industry has already been put on alert with respect to the safety of consumers.

The FDA has moved to create a board to review drug safety, but that step has been criticized as not going far enough. In the meantime, the industry has pledged a review of its marketing methods.

Overview of Jobs and Career Paths

CHAPTER 5

Biopharma Sales and Marketing

Most companies consider sales and marketing to be one function, but with two basic areas of activity. Within the Sales function, you can typically find three career tracks: field sales, sales management, and managed markets. A fourth track, sales training, is closely associated with sales and is distinct from the broader training and development function, which is usually associated with human resource departments. Sales training groups bridge the sales and marketing function: in some companies, they are considered part of marketing support, and hence part of the marketing function.

Within the marketing function are two main areas of activity: marketing management and marketing support. Marketing management is responsible for introducing products and managing product life cycles. Marketing support is an umbrella-like term that incorporates several distinct groups, some of which are quite large, but all of which serve essentially the same purpose: to provide support services for marketing managers. Depending on the size of the company, the distinction between the two areas may be either blurred or non-existent. Typical marketing support groups include training and development, advertising and promotion, market analysis, customer call center, e-business, and commercialization and strategic planning.

Fully integrated Big Biotech companies have their own sales and marketing infrastructure and essentially the same job classifications with the same responsibilities. Unlike some of their Big Pharma cousins, biotech sales reps are specialty reps, who market products to specific and highly defined patient groups, for example, promoting specialty injectable protein products to specialist physicians (oncologists) treating a narrowly defined condition. This focus contrasts sharply with those Big Pharma reps promoting small-molecule drugs to non-specialist physicians (primary care doctors, internists) providing general medical care to the mass market.

This is a good time to think about embarking on a career in biopharmaceutical sales and marketing, since more biotech-based drugs are moving through the development pipeline. In addition, roles like business development require a foundation in sales (as well as experience in several other functions). Once hired, many companies encourage valued employees to gain such experience,

Visit Vault at **www.vault.com** for insider company profiles, expert advice, career message boards, expert resume reviews, the Vault Job Board and more.

V/\ULT CAREER LIBRARY   57

and incorporate lateral moves in annual career development plans. This is important to know at the outset, since it will make you more proactive in evaluating the many opportunities available in sales and marketing.

Sales Positions: Field Sales, Sales Management and Managed Markets

Field sales

A position in field sales is the entry-level job in the sales function. The main purpose of the field sales force is to promote the company's products to customers—typically solo or small-practice groups of physicians—within an assigned territory. Reps are carefully selected, trained rigorously, and equipped with detailed product information. They should know their products inside out and work hard to understand the medical science on which those products are based. Within field sales are two areas, territory sales and specialty sales.

The entry-level field sales positions are pharmaceutical sales representative and territory sales representative. The next rung is medical specialist or hospital specialist. Specialty sales representatives are the most experienced, often with several years of direct sales under their belt. This job exists in both Big Biotech and Big Pharma companies.

The responsibilities of a pharmaceutical sales rep are well-defined across the industry and fall into three distinct areas of activity. Selling is the main responsibility, and requires reps to sell the company's products within the assigned territory, make product presentations, arrange educational meetings for physicians, and co-promote products (when the company has made co-marketing deals with another company).

Administrative responsibilities require reps to manage the selling process (i.e., prioritize their physician and pharmacy customer lists, take notes on call outcomes, prepare reports to district manager), attend company meetings, manage time effectively by working out optimal sales call schedules, work out territory logistics with team members, maintain expense logs, arrange for catering for lunchtime seminars with medical specialists, organize promotional materials and drug samples, and maintain the company car.

Professional development responsibilities require reps to learn features, benefits, and basic medical science of assigned products; learn about competing products, and their advantages/disadvantages relative to own product; attend professional development training sessions; complete required online training programs; and master selling process and continually refine selling skills.

Generally speaking, cash compensation comprises salary plus bonuses. Base salaries range from $45,000 to $65,000 and bonuses range from 2-16%, based on both individual and team performance. So cash compensation for entry-level sales reps ranges from $42K to $79K.

Key Questions for Field Sales

Am I self-motivated and able to manage my own time?

Sales reps do not go to an office first thing in the morning. They get in their cars and make their sales calls, often completing administrative functions from their cars. This means that they have to be motivated to get up every day and complete their calls, and manage their time accordingly.

Am I competitive enough to meet specified sales goals?

Sales jobs are structured about specific revenue goals set by managers. In pharmaceuticals, that translates to the number of prescriptions obtained (usually called "scrips" by insiders), since reps close sales by obtaining commitments from physicians. Competing means stretching yourself to meet these goals, which are often aggressive.

Can I handle rejection and disappointment?

This is a key personality trait, since most physicians have very little time to interact with drug reps. Some may be curt; others may simply refuse to see you. If you can keep your ego and drive intact, you'll likely be successful in sales.

Do I like learning about sophisticated scientific products?

The credibility of pharmaceutical reps depends partly on how fluent they are in explaining their product's features and benefits to physicians. Further, they are expected to have a basic knowledge of the medical science on which the product is based. This can sometimes involve some fairly complex concepts, especially with the newer biotech products. Companies put their reps through rigorous training programs that have honest-to-goodness tests that they must

Visit Vault at **www.vault.com** for insider company profiles, expert advice, career message boards, expert resume reviews, the Vault Job Board and more.

V/\ULT CAREER LIBRARY   **59**

pass in order to be permitted into the field. (Testing is standard practice throughout the industry and protects both the company and rep from the consequences of misrepresenting a product's therapeutic effects.) If you think this is a source of stress for young reps, you're right. Putting a positive spin on the prospect of studying and test-prepping in mid-summer, when you'd rather be using your downtime to take in the sun, you'll feel ever so much better when you earn the confidence of your company to represent its products, and even better when physicians come to see you as a valuable source of new product information.

Sales management

Like field reps, the responsibilities of a sales manager fall into three distinct categories. Management responsibilities require a sales manager to lead assigned sales district in meeting upper management goals; recruit, hire and train sales reps; ensure efficient coverage of their assigned geographic area; plan and lead meetings to review sales achievements; and oversee reps' activities when coordinating educational events (e.g., symposia, speakers bureaus, seminars, etc.). Note that reps themselves do the actual event planning and coordination, with the sales manager providing guidance in identifying speakers, determining the scheduling of events, ensuring symposia have needed resources, etc.

Administrative responsibilities require sales managers to develop business plans and plans of action (POAs), implement market strategies, monitor progress of ongoing sales activity, stay current on industry and company issues that impact the sales force, ensure optimal distribution and consistent stocking of product samples, monitor the district's budget, and control its expenses.

Sales managers must also maintain a work environment that maximizes motivation, act as a coach and mentor to the sales reps, and create individualized development plans for each direct report. Cash compensation for sales managers ranges from $82K to $122K.

Key Questions for Sales Management

Do I like to delegate work?

This is one of the keys to management success, since managers work to motivate, coordinate, and persuade others to get results, which is a different intellectual orientation than doing the work (any work) yourself. Companies have career tracks for both managers and skilled specialists (e.g., scientists). Much prestige (and monetary reward) is attached to the management track.

Do I like the power and responsibility associated with the control of corporate resources?

At every level of responsibility, managers have increasing power and control of resources such as operating budgets and human resources. But that usually requires the ability to work through people in situations that demand getting the cooperation of people in several functional areas. Depending on your temperament and how you handle resistance, that prospect may or may not be a source of frustration.

Managed markets

Many companies have separate business units to manage the marketing of their products to HMOs (the health maintenance organizations that most employers sign up with to enroll employees in health insurance programs). Each HMO has an account that is managed by a national account manager. Since HMOs are national organizations, managing those accounts requires a similar focus—as opposed to the geographically limited "territory" of a sales rep selling to physicians in private practice. National account managers ensure that the company's products are listed on the HMO formulary—the list of drugs that are approved by the HMO for discounting.

Jobs titles include national account manager, customer marketing manager, managed care manager, and government affairs manager. Responsibilities here fall into two equally critical areas: managing the customer and managing the account. Customer management responsibilities require account managers to build and maintain relationships with key people within the customer organization (e.g., HMO formulary manager); acquire and continually develop understanding of the customer organization, especially its goals, challenges, and unique needs; and influence key persons, for

Visit Vault at **www.vault.com** for insider company profiles, expert advice, career message boards, expert resume reviews, the Vault Job Board and more.

VAULT CAREER LIBRARY 61

example consulting physicians who review new products in therapeutic areas for which the company has a new product they would like to have listed in the formulary; these listings help ensure the company's products are prescribed by physicians.

In addition to ensuring inclusion in the HMOs formulary, account managers must also meet sales goals and market share objectives for priority products; analyze account information (sales revenue, market share, volume, etc.) to identify opportunities and problem areas; create and implement account-specific strategies (e.g., tips on handling specific customers); and collaborate with various in-house functions (field sales, marketing management, legal, finance, state government affairs, strategic pricing and contract management) and other national account teams to achieve company goals. Cash compensation for national account managers ranges from $89K to $123K.

Key Questions for Managed Markets

Do I like analyzing complex information involving large sums of money and working primarily with one corporate customer?

Managed markets accounts involve large numbers, since HMOs purchase in bulk. The work is highly quantitative. Because bulk purchases translate to millions of dollars in revenue, managed markets accounts have less room for error, and hence, are staffed by professionals with proven experience. Those revenues influence critical relationships with customers, and account managers must also demonstrate the ability to maintain these customer relationships. Because the "customer" is a corporation, most companies (both biotech and Big Pharma) have teams of people assigned to a single account. That changes the dynamic of the sales process, as team members are assigned different tasks within the account (as opposed to the field rep, who calls on many individual small "customers"—i.e., physicians in small or solo practices).

Would I enjoy financial negotiations, where price and profit margins are under increasing pressure?

Negotiating price with HMOs is one of the key tasks of managed markets sales people. The key is to sell product at a profit. How that happens usually depends on the company's pricing strategy. Most companies provide price incentives, by allowing discounts for larger-volume purchases. The key aptitude here is to have a head for numbers, a cool demeanor, and a desire to problem-solve. With most healthcare delivered through managed care organizations of one form or another, drug companies increasingly rely on their managed markets accounts to get their products to the end consumer.

Marketing: Marketing Management, Marketing Support and Sales Training

Marketing management

Marketing management is where marketing strategy is formulated and implemented, new products introduced, and existing-product lifecycles managed. Until recent years, the marketing function was vertically integrated, meaning that a single ladder existed for reaching senior positions. It was theoretically possible to begin a career as an entry-level marketing associate, and several decades later, achieve senior executive VP for marketing. Some Big Pharma companies are still organized this way.

Yet with Big Pharma companies merging into mega-companies (e.g., Pfizer acquired both Warner-Lambert and Pharmacia to become the largest company in the industry), some companies have opted to organize therapeutic areas and their associated products into separate business units, so that marketing management decisions get made with fewer layers of oversight and with closer contact with customer physicians and targeted patient groups. In this organizational model, therapeutic areas (i.e., oncology drugs, cardiovascular drugs, anti-hypertensives, etc.) and the products associated with them, become wholly integrated business units. Most Big Biotech companies who chose to develop a sales/marketing infrastructure have opted for the second model, since their more-targeted products are best delivered in smaller organizations.

The main job title in marketing management (consistent throughout the industry) is product manager. A product manager's responsibilities fall into two main categories, management and administration. The product manager must develop and manage the short-term product strategy and marketing plans for assigned products, oversee development of business plans, specify the positioning of a product among its competitors, monitor those competitor products, acquire both a quantitative and intuitive feel for customer needs,

Visit Vault at www.vault.com for insider company profiles, expert advice, career message boards, expert resume reviews, the Vault Job Board and more.

VAULT CAREER LIBRARY   63

and act as an in-house champion for a product or brand. Administratively, product managers must develop budgets, maintain records of expenses, and manage and develop entry-level support staff (e.g., market research analysts, marketing associates, undergraduate interns and co-op students, etc.).

In companies where therapeutic areas and associated products are organized as business units, product managers effectively become mini-CEOs, involved in virtually every aspect of getting a product to market. Product managers should also have substantial communication and negotiation skills, as they are required to interact with professionals from every part of the organization. Cash compensation for product managers ranges from $75K to $104K.

Key Questions for Marketing Management

Do I like thinking about ALL the aspects of getting a product to market, including those that require skills I may not have?

Many product managers are drawn from the ranks of people with substantial quantitative skills, since the job requires careful manipulation of price, volume, and venues of distribution. Yet product managers must also oversee the advertising materials for their products, which can require a creative element to enhance the "saleability" of the product.

Do I like the feeling of being a mini-CEO early in my career? Do I like having to interact with ALL manner of people to get my work done?

If yes, then product management may be for you. It's perfectly ok to have a Napoleon complex, as long as it is tempered with a sense of diplomacy and a respect for other professionals. Product managers are at the center of the action. (Note: implicit in this job is the understanding that business hours expand significantly during the hectic periods around product launch time.)

Marketing support: sales training

Most pharmaceutical companies maintain their own sales training departments to train new hires, and continue the training of experienced reps. Sales training groups have a specific mandate to maintain the performance of the sales force, and are therefore highly knowledgeable of the issues and problems facing their student base. Indeed, many field reps spend at least one or more years as classroom trainers to deepen their expertise. Most companies develop at least part of their learning programs in-house, with the balance outsourced to equally specialized sales training consulting companies serving the industry at large.

Sales training jobs include sales trainer, technical training specialist, regional trainer, and national sales trainer, with each title carrying increasing responsibility. Management jobs are typically called sales training managers. Within the group are also other positions, such as instructional designers, project managers, and media specialists, since training is increasingly delivered through technological media such as CDs or on Web sites. Typically, such programs are highly modularized and completed on the sales reps' personal time.

Sales training usually requires several years of experience as a field sales rep to break in. Most companies tap their best field sales reps to become trainers. Sales trainers plan, organize and manage the programs needed to bring newly hired reps in line with the company's products and sales process.

A sales trainer's responsibilities fall into three categories: training delivery, administrative, and professional development. Trainers must conduct on-site training sessions within his assigned geographic area (this could be either a district or larger geographic region), manage the self-study portion of training programs, conduct generic selling skills programs as well as new-hire training programs. Self-study learning programs typically have highly technical basic science and extensive product knowledge modules.

Traditionally, this training component was delivered in massive, self-study binders containing hundreds of pages of information. More recently, this same material has been put into Web-based sites or alternatively, on CDs. Since companies expect studying to occur during off-work hours, the newer formats enable reps to access information in discrete chunks at their convenience. Self-study programs also contain testing which trainers administer; trainers also track student performance and ultimately evaluate a rep's readiness to present to physician customers. So a trainer's role is rich in responsibility and consequence.

Beyond self-study, trainers apply all manner of tools, ranging from contests to competitive games to role-play exercises, in workshops and other in-class learning events designed to develop the verbal, presentation, and sales skills of their reps. These learning experiences represent one of the most creative parts of the trainer's job.

Visit Vault at **www.vault.com** for insider company profiles, expert advice, career message boards, expert resume reviews, the Vault Job Board and more.

VAULT CAREER LIBRARY   **65**

Administrative responsibilities include evaluating trainees and communicating performance information to training management. An important third duty is to ensure reps understand and comply with company and industry policies, especially the all-important Pharmaceutical Industry Code of Ethics for promoting its products to physicians. This code limits the total value of gifts made to physicians and restricts the subsidies provided physicians to attend educational events sponsored by the rep's company. Company policies may recognize limits placed by the FDA on the promotion of a company's product to certain at-risk patient populations.

Sales trainers also spend some time developing themselves and their peers. Professional development typically involves setting up, attending, or managing "train-the-trainer" sessions. These are learning events focused on building trainers' classroom delivery skills, and involve much meticulous planning, testing and refining. Professional development duties also include networking among peers to develop contacts and to learn about other company products. Cash compensation for sales training managers ranges from $79K to $121K.

Key Questions for Sales Training

Do I enjoy teaching?

This is a fundamental question that you can answer early on, often while still in college by volunteering to tutor in a favorite subject or serving as a teaching assistant for a professor. Teaching, it is said, is one of the best ways to truly master a subject.

Do I like helping others develop their expertise?

Most people who choose sales as a career enjoy interacting with people. Some decide that they prefer this aspect of sales-related work without the relentless pressure of meeting sales goals. Others, however, do stints in training as a career development step, spending a year or two as trainers before moving on to sales management or marketing management. Whatever your motivation, developing experience in training will distinguish you from your peers and expose you to one of the most people-oriented jobs in the industry.

Am I comfortable speaking to a group day in, day out?

Unlike university professors, who do classroom teaching one or two hours at a time, trainers present day-long programs for several days at a time. Companies structure training days tightly, with little down time, and require the full attention, as trainers are evaluated at the end of the session. (Evaluations ensure that learning days—which take reps away from the field, and therefore, the sales arena—yield maximum learning.) So trainers need to be as fresh during the last hour of the last day as the first.

Do I like to take complex information covering scientific, legal, regulatory, and market issues and present it in engaging, creative ways?

Executing creative learning activities takes work, especially when dealing with thorny subjects like regulatory problems, responding to physician issues and objections, or describing your product's positioning statement. You'll need equal parts analytical, creative, and interpersonal skills to thrive in a sales trainer's job.

Marketing support: advertising and promotion

Advertising and promotion groups produce the many "marketing collateral" materials that describe a product's purpose and function to physicians. Specific areas of expertise include promotion management, professional education programs, consumer relationship marketing, advertising media services, systems support, and creative services.

Often slick and expensive to produce, these materials are a major cost to pharmaceutical companies, but key to how customers perceive products. As with training departments, actual production may occur both in-house or be outsourced to specialist advertising companies, which bid on specific Big Pharma accounts and support the industry as a whole. In the latter case, in-house staff oversees off-site development, ensuring ad copy and media materials accurately portray product positioning statements, proven therapeutic effects, and intended targeted patient population.

Job titles include advertising coordinator, copyeditor, media buyer, advertising/promotion specialist, brand manager, and advertising/promotion manager. Compensation for an entry-level advertising coordinator ranges from $44K to $65K.

Visit Vault at **www.vault.com** for insider company profiles, expert advice, career message boards, expert resume reviews, the Vault Job Board and more.

VAULT CAREER LIBRARY   67

Key Questions for Advertising and Promotion

Am I visually oriented?

Because Big Pharma companies target physician groups, the bulk of their print ads are inserted in professional journals and trade publications. These inserts contain all the information described above and must be visually engaging. In recent years, direct-to-consumer television ads have gained in popularity. These aim to boost sales by inducing the end consumer to prompt her physician to consider prescribing the advertised drug for the condition that prompted the physician visit. Whether in print or media, a knack for presenting medical information in attention-grabbing ways is a must for this work area.

Do I have enough of a business orientation to understand the advertising bottom line?

The purpose of advertising is to sell—plain and simple. Some people in the creative world tend to lose sight of that. Remembering advertising's larger business context will serve you well. For medical advertising, particularly now that the DTC is under increased scrutiny, the challenge is to present the product's potential in treating a disease condition, while being transparent about its adverse or negative effects and which population segments should not consume the product.

Marketing support: market analysis

Market analysis groups are responsible for gathering and analyzing business information in specific geographic areas to understand the economic profile of specific disease conditions in which the company specializes, the associated targeted patient populations—including demographic trends and shifts and progression of disease conditions—and the competitive landscape for the products under development. Jobs titles include market analyst and regional analyst.

A market analyst's responsibilities are consistent throughout the industry: performing local healthcare marketplace assessments, provide analysis and consulting support to sales and marketing management, developing and implementing tools and processes for standard sales performance measurement, identifying opportunities and assessing threats for the company's products, measuring financial ratios (e.g., return on investment or

ROI, market share, etc.), and analyzing tactical plans based on historic performance. Cash compensation for entry-level market research analysts ranges from $39K to $50K.

Key Questions for Market Analysis

Am I comfortable manipulating hoards of data to identify what's happening in the marketplace?

Market analysts need to have excellent quantitative skills as well as an ability to interpret that data into concise conclusions about how a market is changing. For example, are the demographics in a geographic area are shifting to say, older people, that will translate into an across-the-board increase in pharmaceutical consumption. Alternatively, are more people from a specific ethnic or racial group entering that same area? Given the prevalence of certain disease conditions in some groups more than others, the demand for products to address those conditions will likely increase. Market analysts tease out such shifts and feed their conclusions to marketing management.

Am I comfortable with specialized software programs that interpret market data?

Many companies build customized applications on top of commercial, number-crunching, analytical products, which require understanding of the basic products, such as SAS or SPSS and some additional learning to master the in-house components.

Marketing support: customer call center

Customer call centers provide the first line of support for patients and consumers seeking information about a company's product. A customer support representative's (CSR's) responsibilities typically involve dealing with customer issues, gathering customer feedback, and analyzing customer data. Customer-related responsibilities are to apply selling and product knowledge to complete sales calls made through interactive video desktop computers, resolve physician-customer complaints and issues, build relationships with physicians, and nurture physician loyalty.

Analysis-related responsibilities are to identify and collect adverse event information and analyze trends for management. The latter is particularly important for pharmaceutical companies, since it helps companies keep a pulse on targeted physician customers and end consumer patient groups.

Visit Vault at **www.vault.com** for insider company profiles, expert advice, career message boards, expert resume reviews, the Vault Job Board and more.

VAULT CAREER LIBRARY   69

CSRs should always maintain a strong customer focus. In this context, it means making sure internal customers, such as marketing managers and sales managers, and external customers, such as physicians or pharmacists, get the information they need to analyze both therapeutic effects and consumer preferences. Cash compensation for entry-level call center reps ranges from $23K to $33K, but goes up significantly with experience.

Key Questions for Customer Call Center

Do I like interacting with people through technology?

Some people are more comfortable relating to others if they do not actually see them. If you are such a person, then customer service may be for you. Don't get the mistaken idea that customer call support is low-level work being outsourced to the poorer reaches of the planet. Time-pressed customer physicians may very well prefer to get introduced to new products through this vehicle—albeit often at hours that are convenient for them.

Do I have the communication skills intrinsic to a job that requires complex information to be delivered by telephone?

This job requires that you do a lot of talking. That may seem like employment heaven to the extroverted among us, but positively intimidating to introverts. A hefty dose of patience and intelligence are also pluses, since companies get calls from people in all manner of moods asking for information that requires a basic understanding of the medical science behind a product and that product's characteristics. One key to success here is to never leave a caller with an unsatisfied need, even if that means referring him to others in the group.

Marketing support: commercialization and strategic planning

Most biotech companies and many pharmaceutical companies have commmmercialization groups dedicated to ensuring the smooth entry of products into the marketplace. These groups plan product launches, set launch priorities, coordinate with training services, arrange consumer marketing and complete the many other steps involved in the product commercialization process. Planning product launches requires huge logistical efforts, as companies launch products simultaneously in many geographic areas. Commercialization groups maintain databases containing records of the company's institutional experience in launching its products, so as to leverage the learning from each experience to ensure a more efficient process in subsequent launches.

Jobs include strategic planner and product launch support specialist, but these titles have broad variation throughout the industry. What is consistent is the essential marketing support nature of the responsibilities. Because job titles vary, it is difficult to pinpoint compensation, but it ranges from $75K to $105K.

Key questions for Commercialization and Strategic Planning

Do I like to chart courses, see the big picture, and help define which products get to the marketplace?
Strategic planning requires a "big picture" comprehension of the business environment, which is difficult to get early on in a career. The other aspect of strategic planning is that it requires a sound understanding of a product's economic potential.

Would I prefer thinking about a product's business potential or its scientific properties?
Many technically-oriented people are more at home investigating a molecule's scientific properties and medical effects than analyzing its potential value in the marketplace. Having an honest understanding of where you land on this question will go a long way toward making clear-headed career decisions. For better or worse, however, the overall trend in business organizations is for everyone in the enterprise to become engaged in one way or another in the value-creating outputs of the organization.

E-business

E-business jobs involve setting up and maintaining e-commerce web sites, which are often hidden from the public at large. These business-to-business (B2B) sites facilitate the purchase of bulk volumes of pharmaceuticals to

Visit Vault at **www.vault.com** for insider company profiles, expert advice,
career message boards, expert resume reviews, the Vault Job Board and more.

VAULT CAREER LIBRARY   71

large pharmacy groups. They also provide transaction support to distributors and end-retailers.

The most important responsibility of an e-business analyst is to ensure the company's optimal utilization of the Internet as a sales and distribution channel. The e-business group's core responsibilities are to research, design and maintain web sites that promote the company's products, develop customized Web applications, and continually improve the interactivity of the various sites.

Note that these B2B sites are distinct from general information and educational sites, which contain product descriptions, clinical trial results, FDA rulings, disease condition information, and other material of interest to targeted patient groups and their associated advocacy groups. Jobs include e-business analyst or e-commerce market analyst. Cash compensation ranges from $57K to $79K.

Key Questions for E-business

Do I think the Web is the IT place to be in the business world?

This is another tech-intensive job that is being increasingly recognized as an important distribution channel. The sheer efficiency of the Web in completing transactions is reason enough for companies to set up sites that allow e-transactions. Traditional brick-mortar operations have now become click-and-mortar.

Do I want direct contact with people or am I more attracted to analyzing electronic transactions?

Transactions are manifested as incoming data on a computer screen. The world of e-business needs people who are perfectly happy interpreting their requests through well, a screen. This work area collects all manner of business information—who customers are, where they live, what products they purchase, the dollar volume of those purchases, and occasionally, what irritates them. Millions of bits of such data are collected and digested by e-business analysts, who must identify trends in the marketplace, what is causing changes in those trends, and to what extent they will impact each component of the business transaction.

GETTING HIRED

Educational Requirements and Internships

CHAPTER 6

Requirements by Position

All jobs in sales and marketing require at least a BA/BS degree, and advanced degrees, such as MBAs, are preferred for some job classifications (e.g., product management). Other functional areas, notably manufacturing or operations, have job classes that that do not require that benchmark. Nonetheless, biopharma is one of the most knowledge-intensive industries, and most companies expect to continue to invest heavily in the professional development of their employees. We've already talked about having to earn passing grades on product training tests before being permitted to represent the company's products to physician customers.

Whatever the work area, candidates should demonstrate a knowledge foundation in the life sciences. Majors in biology, biochemistry, bioengineering, biophysics, plant biology, organic chemistry, medicinal chemistry, molecular biology, computational biology, and genetics are most valuable. Larger schools with extensive course offerings have separate majors in these areas, while smaller schools offer specific courses in broader subject areas, such as biology or chemistry. Other backgrounds, such as nursing, are also valuable and can be transitioned into several careers in the industry.

Unless a job requires a specific license—such as an MD to practice medicine—most employers include clauses such as "or equivalent experience" at the end of the required qualifications section of job listings. This prevents the exclusion of candidates with unusual backgrounds or ones who may not have acquired formal academic credentials. Many people opt to obtain advanced degrees while holding down full-time jobs.

Field sales

A BS degree is required to break into field sales. Although field rep is the entry-level sales job, many companies prefer to see some evidence of sales or sales-related experience before hiring someone in that position. If you're wondering how to get experience before you've even finished your college education, rest assured that most companies are quite flexible in this requirement and usually accept sales-related experience acquired in a broad range of industries.

The thinking is that, after a year or two of daily exposure to the sales process, people either become acclimated to the structure, pacing, and risk of rejection that come with professional sales or opt out for another field. Those who make that critical first self-selected cut become the most attractive candidates. Upon being hired, they will already have a foundation in selling skills—in addition to that knowledge base.

Summers, part-time, or between semesters are all legitimate periods where you can get sales jobs. Promoting your favorite sports equipment, for example, will expose you to a retail environment and to meeting customer needs. But, we hope you'll be more adventurous. Remember, selling pharmaceuticals is selling a product that humans will consume, and as such, its promotion has a higher level of risk associated with it. Hence, the training, tests, and ultra-tight control over the message. To get exposure, try related areas—for example, medical devices, hospital supplies, nutritional supplements, pharmacy products, over-the-counter drugs, and other healthcare maintenance products directed at consumers. Targeting these related areas to get that initial sales experience will broaden your perspective and demonstrate your focus. Alternatively, you'll find out fairly quickly—and with a minimal cost to your career—that selling is not satisfying to you.

In order to avoid that downer, make full use of the many self-assessments (e.g., Myers Briggs Personality Inventory) available through the career services offices of most colleges and universities. Be sure you get a good idea, as well, of which jobs are best suited for a given temperament.

The people you'll be competing with for field sales position will likely include one or two with substantial experience who have decided to make a career transition. For example, many nurses experience burnout and opt for pharma sales careers. Alternatively, some PhD level researchers opt to become medical liaison officers, a relatively new pharma sales job classification, rather than continue in laboratory research. In these cases, companies may overlook a lack of previous sales experience since the candidate brings additional depth in other areas. It may hardly seem fair to have to compete with somebody with 10 or 15 years of experience, but companies have learned that such diversity encourages dynamism, as people bring different talents to the table. The important thing is to be aware of the value you bring and to dedicate yourself to enhancing that value.

Sales management

As with field sales, sales management positions require at least an undergraduate degree, preferably in a natural or life science. The entry-level sales management job is district sales manager. Although it is not essential to have an MBA to land a job on that first rung of the management ladder, many recently promoted field reps decide to pursue MBAs while working as district managers.

Many companies sponsor promising managers in MBA programs. Other companies grow their own business leaders by developing customized, in-house programs that focus on the specific challenges of their industry and groom student-managers to senior leadership positions.

District sales manager jobs are typically filled by candidates with several years of experience in the field sales force, but this is not an exclusive rule. Candidates may also come from any of several groups within either the sales or marketing areas, including product management, sales training, or market analysis. In many cases, companies permit people to complete one to two year rotations, i.e., periods where they leave their main career track to gain exposure in a vital area—in this case, sales management—in order to broaden their professional exposure before returning to their main career.

Managed markets

Working in managed markets requires the same baseline BS degree, but many companies want a master's degree in systems analysis or statistics, with many expressing a preference toward the MBA, ostensibly for the business context. Undergraduate degrees can be in any of the natural or life sciences.

Moving into managed markets requires well-developed technological expertise in systems analysis, database, customer relationship management (CRM) applications, decision sciences (particularly decision-making under uncertainty), strategic planning, competitive analysis, and financial management. Coursework is available for some of these topics at the undergraduate level, but most topics are covered in graduate coursework. This extensive IT and business foundation is essential, since most accounts are national, enrolling millions of people. Along the way, be sure to cultivate the softer skills—team-selling skills, presentation, oral communication, negotiation—since managed markets accounts are inherently team-oriented.

To break into a position, companies also require three or four years of experience in either field sales or in one of the several groups within

Visit Vault at **www.vault.com** for insider company profiles, expert advice, career message boards, expert resume reviews, the Vault Job Board and more.

V/\ULT CAREER LIBRARY   77

marketing. That sales experience should come with significant account management responsibilities and ideally be focused on business-to-business sales.

Marketing management

Most Big Pharma companies want an MBA to land a position in product management, the core group in marketing management. New MBAs may be hired as assistant product managers, if they bring several years of experience as marketing analysts or sales reps prior to attending business school. With those two sets of credentials, the exact nature of the undergraduate major becomes less important. In recent years, Big Pharma companies have required a scientific foundation of some kind, meaning majors in chemistry, biochemistry, biology, and similar fields. Big Biotech companies require an undergraduate degree in a life science, especially in areas like molecular biology, genetics, physiology, etc.

Product managers should also have a multitude of "soft" skills. Be sure to include courses that will help you develop skills in negotiation, social psychology, decision-making, and leadership development. To develop the "hard" skills, select courses that give you plenty of practice number-crunching, working with database software programs, and understanding internet commerce. Finally, be sure you know the difference between "big picture" strategic thinking and nitty-gritty details of research studies. When possible, select courses requiring case analysis, since the problems many cases address require both types of thinking to solve. A staple of MBA programs, many undergraduate courses incorporate at least one or two cases in their syllabi.

Marketing support: sales training

Sales trainers typically begin their careers as field reps. You'll need at least a BS degree in a life science and at least three or four years of pharmaceutical sales experience to get into a training position. Most companies will also want you to demonstrate good presentation and group facilitation skills.

Successful candidates should be thoroughly familiar with both the therapeutic area and the product being promoted. Training positions place a premium on presentation and communication skills. Good trainers also have empathy and are able to establish a connection with their students easily. Although fear of failure is a great motivator for newly hired sales reps, better trainers provide a positive motivation via the enthusiasm with which they present their material.

Marketing support: advertising and promotion

Beyond the needed BS, successful candidates will need to demonstrate writing and editing skills. People who aspire to management positions in this area should strongly consider business education, and many people opt for MBAs. But other relevant master's degrees, such as in communications, are also valued.

One possible route to a job in a Big Pharma company is to work in a medical advertising firm or an ad agency with a group dedicated to pharmaceutical accounts. This is a special niche within the advertising world, since the content of the copywriting is scientific in nature and the customer audience is usually specialized physicians. You may well wonder who makes those DTC ads and how the debate over Cox-2 inhibitors will impact ad creation. In early 2005, both pharmaceutical and ad agency executives are revising their approach to DTC ads. In addition, internet-based advertising is likely to continue to grow.

Marketing support: market analysis

Market Analyst jobs are by nature quantitative. In recent years, BS degrees in functional business areas, such as marketing, have become available. This is by far the most directly relevant undergraduate major, although a broader business major is also acceptable. In addition to marketing-oriented coursework, be sure to pick up courses in statistics, operations research, and quantitative decision science. Be sure you are thoroughly familiar with designing and implementing market research studies and have mastered the tools needed to interpret data.

Most companies require four or five years of experience, preferably within the industry, before hiring someone with a BS. That experience can include any combination of roles, including field sales rep, marketing associate, associate product manager, or market analyst.

Obtaining an MA/MS in any of the fields cited is a smart step, although most companies will also need to see several years of experience. It is possible to work toward that master's degree while on the job, and many people choose that route. Many people opt for MBAs, which are more general in nature that master's degrees in specialized fields and open doors to management jobs.

Visit Vault at **www.vault.com** for insider company profiles, expert advice, career message boards, expert resume reviews, the Vault Job Board and more.

V/\ULT CAREER LIBRARY   **79**

Demonstrating an understanding of the industry is critical in landing a job. Since most pharmaceutical companies want experience first, where should you break in? Consider analyst jobs in allied fields, such as consumer healthcare products or medical devices.

In addition, while still in college, focus term projects on issues relevant to the industry or that require you to research companies and their products. For example, if your statistics course requires a term project, consider analyzing epidemiological data on contemporary diseases, such as HIV/AIDS or any of the many cancers afflicting the U.S. population. Better yet, inquire about acting as an Assistant to a professor, whose research focuses on healthcare information. Collecting healthcare data through primary sources, such as surveys, provides valuable experience in working with survey results; secondary sources, such as government agency databases, will give you industry contacts and are yet another way to get some exposure.

Marketing support: customer call center

Most pharmaceutical companies require their customer service reps to have a college degree, usually a BS, but have provisions for people with some college and "equivalent" experience. The qualifier is meant to avoid excluding older workers, who entered the workforce before the current academic requirement was implemented, or workers who are returning to the workforce after a long absence, yet who have ample practical job experience. If you are on track for a bachelor's degree, you can fast-forward to the next paragraph. If you entered the workforce after earning an associate of science degree some years ago, you'll want to take advantage of company-sponsored education programs to enhance your skills.

If you are just entering the workforce, you'll also need a year or two of sales experience to become an attractive candidate to a Big Pharma company. Ideally, that experience should have been in settings requiring direct contact with customers—i.e., the retail level. In contrast with CSRs for most consumer products companies, those working for Big Pharma companies not only provide product utilization and adverse effects information to patients, but also complete sales transactions, make online presentations, and give specialized information on new products to physicians. It is this broader mandate that raises the bar for entry qualifications.

You can get that needed experience relatively easily by finding work in retail sales, selling anything from nutritional supplements to health-enhancing devices to healthcare supplies. Even part-time work counts. Remember, companies want to be sure you've gotten your feet wet learning basic selling skills before they ply you with their own product information.

Reps need to have good organizational skills and be comfortable spending long periods in front of a computer screen. Customer service reps should expect to spend considerable study time boning up on product knowledge provided in company-sponsored training programs.

Marketing support: e-Business

e-Business analysts almost always have an MS degree. Most companies require undergraduate majors in computer science and would like to see Master's level education. Master of science degrees in computer science, applied mathematics, or systems analysis are acceptable. Many companies would like to see some business education as well, usually at the master's level. MBA programs in the management of technology or internet commerce are quite attractive.

Marketing support: commercialization and strategic planning

Strategic planners need education at the master's level. As with e-business, many companies have some flexibility in the specific type of degree. For undergraduate work, majors may be in any of the physical, life sciences, or bio-engineering. This breadth reflects the breadth of applications. For example, a medical device company will find an undergraduate degree in bio-engineering most useful, whereas a biotech company will be attracted to the same degree in molecular biology.

Because commercialization involves getting products ready for launch, companies need people with many different skill sets. Often, people move into this inherently inter-disciplinary area after working in a specialized functional area for several years. Since there is no one-size-fits-all education target, there are several examples of master's level majors that have industry applications in commercialization and strategic planning. MBAs in operations management with specific skills in project management, logistics planning, and supply chain management are most useful. Facility with the tools of finance and accounting is also expected.

Within these groups, you will also find at least one research-trained PhD who is responsible for the early stages of commercialization. This usually involves being in charge of producing scaled-up quantities of products and

Visit Vault at **www.vault.com** for insider company profiles, expert advice, career message boards, expert resume reviews, the Vault Job Board and more.

V/\ULT CAREER LIBRARY   **81**

interfacing with the R&D group. The small percentage of laboratory oriented PhDs who go on to earn MBAs are attractive candidates for companies looking to staff this group.

Education Programs

Pharmaceutical companies will accept degrees from any accredited college or university. Most institutions offer undergraduate degrees in business, which can be further concentrated into any of the core areas—finance, accounting, marketing, etc. Within this context, most programs expose students to case studies from a broad range of industries to give as broad an exposure to the business world as possible. Students who have identified the industry in which they want to spend their career can further focus their studies by doing term projects and other papers on issues within that industry.

If you plan to apply for a pharmaceutical sales position with only a BA/BS, you will gain a competitive edge by demonstrating an understanding of the key issues facing the industry—e.g., pricing, drug reimportation, broader access to underprivileged groups, among others—in an interview. Even more critical is to become aware of the positions developed by industry leaders. The best place to learn about industry issues is from the trade group, PhRMA's Web site, which contains detailed explanations on major issues, including generics, intellectual property protection, pricing, availability of drugs, etc. You may have strong feelings about how companies should (or should not) promote their products to consumers, but be conscious of separating fact from feeling in preparing for an interview. Be able to articulate specific issues, how the industry plans to deal with them, and alternative perspectives in the media and patient advocacy community. To really distinguish yourself, be sure to read up on available options and the trade-offs involved in adopting each one.

A few higher education institutions have developed industry-specific undergraduate and graduate degrees. These programs provide a customized talent pool for the industry but are by no means required to land a job.

Academic Program	Description
University of the Sciences, Philadelphia (UPS), PA **(www.usip.edu/pcp/)**	USP's primary focus is in the health professions and sciences; has programs at all academic levels: undergraduate, professional, and graduate. Two programs at the BS level: • Pharmaceutical Marketing and Management • Pharmaceutical Sciences Programs for both MBA and Executive MBA level: • Pharmaceutical Business Many pharmaceutical companies are located in the mid-Atlantic states (NY, PA, NJ), making the Philadelphia location particularly convenient.
Rutgers (The State University of New Jersey), Camden, Newark and New Brunswick, NJ campuses **(business.rutgers.edu/)**	Like USP, Rutgers' proximity to Big Pharma companies has created the impetus for several programs. Check out the Continuing Education Program, which profiles the pharmaceutical sales rep job along several dimensions: education, specialized subject knowledge, required skills, and transferable skills. This is a valuable tool that can really help you sort out what you need to learn to land an offer. Example: • Education: Marketing/Sales—Undergraduate Degree • Knowledge: Sales Strategy • Skills: Selling Techniques Within the several MBA programs are these relevant concentrations: • Biotechnology Commercialization • Pharmaceutical Management

Visit Vault at **www.vault.com** for insider company profiles, expert advice, career message boards, expert resume reviews, the Vault Job Board and more.

VAULT CAREER LIBRARY   **83**

Academic Program	Description
The Erivan K. Haub School of Business at St. Joseph's University, Philadelphia, PA (www.sju.edu/hsb/graduate.htm)	This institution's Jesuit roots emphasize excellence in education within a context of faith and responsibility. Like USP, it has developed an industry-focused MBA to serve the need for graduate education in the area. At the MBA level: • Pharmaceutical Marketing MBA
University of Mississippi, University, MS (Yes, this is the actual name of the town.) (www.rx.olemiss.edu/)	Far from any of the major centers of action, "Ole Miss" offers programs focusing on several aspects of the industry. Within the Department of Pharmacy, lies the Center for Pharmaceutical Marketing and Management, which covers everything from pharmacy entrepreneurship to pharmaceutical marketing research to international pharmaceutical marketing at all levels (BS, MS, PhD). The sheer breadth of offerings makes this a worthwhile program to investigate.

A decision to focus a college-level degree on any one industry is a serious one indeed. The upside is that you'll look very attractive to a hiring manager who wants pre-screened candidates who can hit the ground running. The downside is that you'll be locking in your future within a set of brackets that will be difficult to remove later on if you change careers or industries.

At the graduate level, especially if one or several years have passed since college, zeroing in on a specific industry will help focus both your studies and job search after graduation.

A new choice for non-research careers

To get a job, you need experience, but you won't have experience unless you get a job. Some of the jobs described in this book require at least a year— and usually several years—of experience to break in. That can leave you wondering just how to move forward.

If you are certain that you want to work in biotech and pharmaceuticals and are equally sure you'd rather pass on PhD-level research, check out the recently organized Professional Science Master's or PSM degree, which combines science and business. With a scant half-dozen years of existence, this program is expanding rapidly in colleges and universities willing to experiment with a new concept. Although the most elite institutions—

including Ivy League schools like Harvard and Princeton—have shown a marked resistance to the degree, nevertheless some 900 students are currently enrolled in 45 institutions throughout the U.S.

Within a PSM program, you can further concentrate in specific fields, such as bioinformatics, biotechnology, business and patent law, or financial mathematics. After completing core courses with graduate students, PSM students move on to industry internships or work in business school-like teams on projects dealing with management issues facing current leaders of companies. For example, one project might involve creating a new advertising campaign for a product to be launched in the post-Vioxx world; the team must put together a program that emphasizes educating patients on the disease state and highlighting the benefits of the company's product, while clearly pointing out possible adverse effects. The key is to represent the product fairly, paying careful attention to avoid claiming benefits that have not been demonstrated in the clinical trials data.

PSM students embark on this pragmatic aspect of their programs about the same time PhD students begin their dissertation-based laboratory research. The typical PSM graduate is 24 years old and starts out earning $55K in business or $45K in government.

The Sloan Foundation and the W.M. Keck Foundation have together donated over $60 million in grants to get the PSM degree program going. In addition—and also in contrast to traditional academics—foundation leaders that opted to work closely with industry to identify current and near future staffing needs, something that traditional academics usually shun.

The main criticism of PSM programs is that they lack the intellectual rigor of original research. Moreover, that industry tie can make the degree more vulnerable to local economic fluctuations and downturns.

Despite these issues, both the University of North Carolina and California State University are currently considering creating PSM programs, with dozens more likely to follow suit. Ultimately, this is yet another option for obtaining the skills needed for higher-level marketing and administrative jobs in the industry.

Internships

Internships have become a virtually indispensable vehicle for breaking into the industry. The story of how Henry A. McKinnell, CEO of Pfizer, Inc., started is worth noting. His original dream was to become a college professor; he prepared by earning a Ph.D. from Stanford Business School. After a couple of attempts by Pfizer to recruit him, McKinnell finally accepted a position with them, thinking he should get some real-world experience before returning to academia. When questioned about his specific interests, he requested to be assigned to a field sales position, which puzzled his new employer, given his academic background and soft-spoken manner. But that manner belied McKinnell's shrewdness: he knew he needed to have a grip on sales in order to really understand the business. And understand he did. He moved up the sales organization quickly, and earned international experience by running full-scale operations in Asia before returning to Pfizer's New York headquarters for a series of executive positions.

So how do you land one of those internships? Happily, the traditional campus career service center is augmented by Web sites sponsored by companies themselves, trade associations, professional groups, and advocacy groups for various segments of the student population. In addition, international internships are starting to become available and are well worth your while to explore, as the industry is global and it is increasingly looking for candidates with a "global" intellectual perspective. See the appendix for a complete list of internships—company, academic, trade and international.

Resumes and Cover Letters

CHAPTER 7

Overview of Pharma Sales Resumes

Guidance on crafting the content and format of your resume is plentiful. But beware. Most of it is generic, and can be applied across many fields. Your task is to craft the best resume that will land you a specific job—sales—in a scientific industry. This section is another opportunity to take a close look at how well your strengths match with the ideal profile for a top sales performer.

Primary traits for sales success

Self-confident. Above all, sales stars need to be able to handle the stream of rejections that come from physicians not having time to meet with them, not giving more than two or three minutes of attention where 10 or more would have been preferred, outright refusing to see them—even after they've been waiting in the reception room, being short-tempered or cranky, or any number of other quite common circumstances around making those required 8 to 10 calls per day.

Persuasive. Since you will only have three or four minutes to make your pitch, every phrase needs to pull its weight in persuading the physician that your company's product is better than existing alternatives. Given how often you will be called upon to apply this trait, you should enjoy being persuasive and look forward to refining your presentation to achieve this end.

Self-starter. Remember, reps do not punch clocks and have no one overseeing when they start their day. You get up, get into your car, and make your calls. You might have to field a call or two from the cell phones of other team members covering your territory, but chances are they are also working to remain consistent in their work habits. This lack of structure requires that you be able to motivate yourself. Companies know that connection is important, and thus, arrange for continual training meetings to give people a chance to meet each other.

Action-oriented. You should have an instinct to act—as opposed to say, deliberate—and thus you will want to be continually out there, figuring out the best way to reach a difficult physician or refine a presentation. From ongoing actions, you can then learn what is working and what is not. With

Visit Vault at **www.vault.com** for insider company profiles, expert advice, career message boards, expert resume reviews, the Vault Job Board and more.

V/\ULT CAREER LIBRARY **87**

an action-orientation, your efforts will produce ample empirical field data and observations, which effectively become the basis on which in-house analysts will determine what is happening in the market.

Competitive. You should be perpetually conscious of how well you are doing relative to your peers and to an absolute goal and you should be energized, rather than stressed, by the presence of another competitive person entering your team. In fact, competition is a way of life, a way of seeing the world, with scores—either in dollars or sports measures—a way of letting you know how you are doing. If you come up short in a competitive contest and your attitude hovers around "I'll get there next time," then you'll probably get to Fridays with enough energy to enjoy your weekend. If, on the other hand, the same event craters your self-esteem and leaves you introspective, it's more likely the weekly drive to meet sales goals will create unrelenting stress.

Goal-directed. You measure achievement in highly concrete ways. That keeps you on track here, but ironically, can be frustrating in pharmaceuticals because of the way the selling process works. Sales people never actually exchange goods for money in the closing. Once they obtain a commitment from the physician, it can be up to three months before reps actually see their territory's sales data. That becomes delayed gratification, which, in turn, requires even more goal-directedness to make it to the next cycle.

Need to be heard. Also described as the ability to take charge, to be in command, to have one's point of view listened to and understood. Because face time with the customer (the physician) is so limited, top sales people need to have a strong urge to convey their information, whatever the obstacles. Note that pharmacists are also customers, and many reps arrange to make a couple of calls to pharmacists before going to see physicians, since the former has greater accessibility than the latter.

Secondary traits for sales success

Ability to communicate complex information. You'll need to be thoroughly conversant in the science behind the products you are selling, essential if both busy physicians are going to be willing to give up time from their practice to listen to reps' pitches, and for the credibility of the rep.

Attentive to detail. Planning those eight to 10 daily calls requires understanding the geography of the territory and mapping the most efficient routes possible. Each call requires meticulous follow-up notes in the rep's planning book, recording physician comments, special needs, the outcome of the call, and the goal for the next call. Finally, reps carry boxes of product samples to give to physicians, who are willing to prescribe a product on a limited basis to see how it works on their patients before committing to sustained prescribing. Samples are also part of a company's promotion effort. Reps are required to undertake regular inventories and submit the data back to their marketing departments.

Resume Content

Contact information

Include your name, current address, home and mobile telephone numbers, and e-mail address. Use dots to separate out the number groupings in your telephone numbers. This is important to avoid confusion if your resume will be reviewed by people overseas, who do not necessarily use the same format. If you are still in college and are uncertain of your post-graduation address, include your permanent address. Avoid post office boxes.

Career objective

This is a carefully crafted phrase that specifies your career goal. If that is pharmaceutical sales, then a simple phrase is all you need. As people grow in their careers, or if they want to make adjustments in direction—say, get into a new group within the same functional area or move to a different functional area—the job is more complex. If you are not sure what specific job or work area you want to target, it is wiser to omit this section altogether.

Skills summary

Along with the objective, the skills summary provides a snapshot of your areas of expertise. Descriptive nouns are used, such as "Negotiation," "account management," and "market research." Many people also include a comprehensive statement of their unique "value proposition." See the sample resumes for examples.

Experience

This is the core of the resume and should be customized for each position as much as possible. To get this right, download and print out a copy of the

Visit Vault at **www.vault.com** for insider company profiles, expert advice, career message boards, expert resume reviews, the Vault Job Board and more.

VAULT CAREER LIBRARY   **89**

required skills listed in the job description, then be sure your bullet lists of experience address the needed skills. Use the key words and phrases included below to describe those accomplishments. See also the sample resumes for examples.

Education

Be explicit about listing your four-year college degree. This is a requirement for employment. Certificates, ongoing coursework, or other non-degree activities may be included here, if they are relevant to achieving your goal. If, for example, you have an undergraduate major in a humanities field and have earned a certificate in a life science, that will count in your favor. For people who want to change careers or make other adjustments in career direction, evidence of training in the new field or other education will demonstrate a willingness to lay a new foundation. Indeed, any evidence of lifelong learning that is professionally related will be helpful. Be careful, however, about including non-professional training, such as bartending or skiing.

Awards and honors

Election to honor societies, such as Phi Beta Kappa or Beta Gamma Sigma, can be mentioned here, as well as scholarships. For experienced professionals, this is the place to include company awards of excellence (e.g., for customer service or team leadership) or citations for community service.

Affiliations

This includes alumni clubs, trade associations, professional groups, etc. that define your peer groups in the workforce. If you are still in college, this is the place to show your involvement in campus clubs and other affinity groups. If you have a leadership position, be sure to mention that as well. Be careful not to include too many clubs and give the impression your attention is so scattered among different activities that you have neither the time nor commitment to devote to your studies.

Skills

This is the place to list your proficiency in specialized computer programs and foreign languages. Be forthright about your real skill level, using markers like "basic, intermediate, and advanced" to qualify your skill level.

With software, most employers assume you have at least basic proficiency in MS Office, so don't include that. Do include programs like SPSS, SQL, Oracle, or the myriad other programs available. These days, foreign language capability is a definite asset.

References

It is assumed that you will have contacted and have available three or four references. Thus, you do not need to mention references in the resume itself.

Key Words		Key Phrases
• Achieved	• Led	• Managed Territory of...
• Attained	• Launched	• Led team of...salespeople to meet department goals
• Awarded	• Maximized	• Increased market share by...
• Captured	• Optimized	
• Communicated	• Persuaded	• Met and exceeded profit margin goal by...percent
• Educated	• Promoted	• Achieved Top Producer status for...reporting periods
• Exceeded	• Prospected	• Sales quota
• Expanded	• Oversaw	
• Generated	• Secured	• Developed key client relationships
• Influenced		• Created client-focused presentations

Resume Sample: Recent College Graduate

John H. Elliot, Jr.

890 Concord Ave. Cambridge, MA 02138
Email: johnhelliot@msn.com
617. 489.2424 (Home) • 617.781.1545 (Mobile)

CAREER OBJECTIVE: Pharmaceutical Sales

PROFILE

Self-motivated problem solver with proven leadership and collaborative abilities. Enthusiastic and able to achieve rapport with prospects easily.

Business Competencies: Customer service; Market Research; Marketing Communications

Management Competencies: Counseling, Listening, Goal setting, Time Management, Team Leadership

EDUCATION

Bachelor of Science, 2003, GPA 3.9
Cambridge College, Cambridge, MA. Major: Biology; Minor: Psychology

PROFESSIONAL EXPERIENCE

Internship, Marketing Research, AstraZeneca,
Westborough, MA Summer 2003

• Developed presentation materials for international anesthesiology conference
• Researched market trends and customer needs for two groups to support launch of new anesthesiology product

Telemarketer, Professional Sales Solutions, Inc.
2001-2002

• Represented manufacturer of health food products
• Exceeded team goals for two consecutive quarters

WORK EXPERIENCE (COLLEGE)

Teaching Assistantship, Freshman Biology Laboratory Course
2003-2004

• Designed and delivered laboratory course for Introduction to Biology

Peer Counselor
2002-2004

• Provided peer-based support for incoming freshman class to facilitate integration into college and house community

AFFILIATIONS
Beta Gamma Sigma (elected 2003)
Undergraduate Student Council (2003-04)

SPECIAL INTERESTS
Team Sports: Skiing, Softball

Resume Sample: Early Career with Some Sales Experience

Deborah C. Rosenberg

1200 Hickory Lane Richmond, VA 23233
Email: deborahcrosenberg@yahoo.com
804. 489.2424 (Home) • 804.781.1545 (Mobile)

CAREER OBJECTIVE: Pharmaceutical Sales

PROFILE

Highly motivated problem solver, with proven track record of sales achievement. Excellent communication and presentation skills.

Consultative Sales; Customer Service; Listening, Goal setting; Training Design and Delivery; Time Management, Team Leadership; Database Analysis

PHARMACEUTICAL SALES PRECEPTORSHIP

Identified and observed pharmaceutical sales representatives with Abbott and Johnson & Johnson, obtaining first-hand exposure to pharmaceutical sales process and the special marketing challenges facing the sales force.

PROFESSIONAL EXPERIENCE

Senior Manufacturer's Representative, Hospital Supplies Corp.
Alexandria, VA 2001-present

• Sold hospital supplies and equipment in the Southeast territory
• Generated over $3 million in sales over employment period, exceeding sales goals for four consecutive quarters
• Earned three letters of commendation for excellent customer service
• Assisted Sales Trainer in developing a consultative approach to selling skills training program for new hires and experienced Reps
• Promoted after second year based on consistently meeting sales goals and on excellent evaluations

Internship, Sales Management, Park, NC
GlaxoSmithKline, Research Triangle Summer 2000

• Provided territory management support to District Manager, including database management and sales data analysis
• Assisted Regional Trainer in delivering new-hire sales force training. Duties included classroom and course materials preparation

EDUCATION

Bachelor of Science, 2001, GPA 3.7
University of Virginia, Charlottesville, VA
Major: Biochemistry
Certificate: Consultative Selling Skills, Selling Excellence Institute

AFFILIATIONS

University of Virginia Alumni Association
Beta Sigma Nu

SKILLS

Languages: French, Spanish; IT: FileMaker Pro

Visit Vault at **www.vault.com** for insider company profiles, expert advice,
career message boards, expert resume reviews, the Vault Job Board and more.

V∧ULT CAREER LIBRARY   93

Resume Sample: Experienced Professional and Career Changer

Gregory L. Dickinson

453 E. 72nd Street, New York, NY 10021
Email: gregoryldickinson@comcast.net
212.895.1050 (Home) • 212.895.2480 (Mobile)

OBJECTIVE: Pharmaceutical Marketing Management

PROFILE

Analytical thinker with proven expertise in engineering processes. Demonstrated leadership ability both within own functional area and across functions. Proven record of innovation as well as creating operational efficiencies. Excellent organizational, communication and presentation skills.

Engineering Analysis, Process Development and Innovation, Team Leadership, Negotiation, Alliance Development, Goal-Setting and Attainment, Cross-functional Collaboration, Client Management

PROFESSIONAL EXPERIENCE

Hoffman-Laroche, Nutley, NJ
Group Leader, Manufacturing Operations, 2000-present

• Managed four groups (up to 25 engineers) within Process Engineering Department
• Responsible for meeting development goals for four groups or up to 10 separate products
• Negotiated alliance agreement with key contract manufacturer, as part of outsourcing of manufacturing of non-core products. Acted as chief point of contact with alliance management. Alliance generated over $1.5 million in savings since its inception in 2003
• Appointed to cross-functional Task Force to explore strategies for reducing the time-to-market for major products. Collaboration created new standards and achieved 20% reduction in time needed
• Acted as chief liaison to Marketing management to analyze product life cycles and optimize ROI of key products. Effort resulted in increase in ROI of 7% on average or $12 million
• Sponsored by company to attend Executive MBA Program at Stern School of Management

Hoffman-Laroche, Nutley, NJ
Chemical Engineer and Senior Chemical Engineer, Manufacturing Operations, 1996-1999

• Developed processes for manufacturing of small molecules for the Process Engineering Group
• Refined procedures developed during Internship, resulting in $1 million savings over 3-yr period
• Earned two Total Quality Management citations for excellence in development techniques
• Appointed as Team Leader for a group of 5 engineers to explore cost-effective ways to manufacture medium-size molecules

Hoffman-Laroche, Nutley, NJ
Internship, Manufacturing Operations, Summer 1995

• Provided process development support for Manager of Process Engineering Department
• Created alternative procedures for the scale-up of a small molecule for Phase II Clinical Trials
• Documented these procedures and analyzed which will give optimal path to required purity levels

EDUCATION

MBA, Marketing, Stern School of Management
New York University, New York, NY

Bachelor of Science, Biomedical Engineering
Columbia College, New York, NY

Resume Sample: Experienced
Professional and Career Changer (cont.)

HONORS AND AWARDS

Beta Gamma Sigma; Merit Scholarships

AFFILIATIONS

Columbia University Alumni Association
New York University Alumni Association

SKILLS

Languages: German; IT: Oracle; Engineering: GMP

Blooper	How to correct it
Unclear academic credentials	The four-year college degree is essential for pharmaceutical sales jobs, although most companies are flexible on the exact field of study. It is not necessary to include the date, although that is acceptable if you are a recent graduate.
	If you are still working toward an undergraduate degree, be sure to state clearly what your education status is at the time the company reviews your resume.
	Bachelor of Arts, Biology Expected Graduation Date: May 2006
Employment gaps	This is especially important if you have several years of experience. The key issue here is to account for your time because it is the quality of your experiences during those periods that will reflect on your values and decisions.
Sloppy appearance	Spell check does not always catch all errors in typing, especially when a word can have two different spellings (note "too" and "two" and "to"). One way to get around this problem is to print out both your resume and cover letter and edit the text the old-fashioned way—with a red pen! Or give your text to a friend, who can bring another set of eyes and a fresh perspective.

Visit Vault at **www.vault.com** for insider company profiles, expert advice, career message boards, expert resume reviews, the Vault Job Board and more.

VAULT CAREER LIBRARY

95

Blooper	How to correct it
Job hopping	There is no hard rule here, but generally, more than three jobs in five years will suggest a lack of stability. This perception, of course, begs the question: lack of stability on whose part, you or the employer? With mergers, downsizing, rightsizing, reorganizing, etc., you may have to change employers more often than you wish. In that case, clearly indicate the reason your tenure was terminated.
	This issue can become a problem if your work experience has been on a project basis, with a couple of long-term contracts and a string of short ones. In such cases, group your clients and develop a single bullet list to showcase your experience.
Extra employment	With pressure on benefits, many people take on second jobs or start part-time businesses. The conventional wisdom is that it is dicey to include this on a resume, as employers can perceive it as a lack of commitment on a full-time level. The underlying issue is one of scattered attention. Careers in pharmaceutical sales are rigorous enough to demand your exclusive attention.

Cover Letters

If you are in the middle of a job search, you may balk at having to create a new cover letter for each prospective employer, but that very customization will add greater focus and specificity to your letter, and hence stand out from those that are obviously form letters. Fortunately, cover letters can be constructed with several standard sections.

Paragraph 1: Introduction

Introduce yourself, including a referring contact or identify the source of a job posting as well as the name of the position to which you are applying. Give a strong reason for your interest in the company and position.

Paragraph 2: Body of letter

This is your chance to define exactly why you should be hired. Referring to the skills and experience specified in the job description, include three or four bullets on how closely your background, experience, and personal qualities match with those of the ideal candidate.

Paragraph 3: Closing

Thank the reviewer for considering your candidacy. Be sure to include an "action step" that will move the process forward. This is usually a request for a face-to-face interview, in which case specifying when you are available and how to contact you will give the reviewer information to consider. It is far more likely, however, that the prospective employer has a set process and timetable and will effectively summon you when he is ready to talk.

A few cover letter pointers

Keep your letter to one page. If you are making an electronic submission, develop a signature that is tasteful and that stands out. Dark, bolded blue in an italic font works well. Avoid funky, hard-to-read fonts and unusual colors. If you are submitting by snail mail, be sure to use fine quality paper, in either white or ivory. However you send your resume and cover letter, be sure to sign the letter!

Cover Letter Sample: Recent College Graduate

Cynthia J. Penn
195 Forrest Street
Watertown, MA 02472
617.926.1933 (Home) • 617.926.5737 (Mobile)

July 17, 2005

Ms. Theresa A. Parker
District Manager
Kennilworth Laboratories, Inc.
1200 Veteran's Place
Westfield, NJ 07090

Dear Ms. Parker,

I am writing to you on the recommendation of Mr. Wallace N. Barton, my Internship manager (Summer 2004) in the marketing department. While working as a marketing research assistant, I had the opportunity to observe first-hand the commitment Kennilworth Laboratories has made to to provide quality pharmaceuticals to the public. Since last summer, I've focused several term projects on the industry and have decided to pursue a career in biopharmaceutical sales and marketing. I am specifically responding to the posting for a pharmaceutical sales representative in last Sunday's New York Times and am attaching my resume for your review.

During college, I built upon my interest in biology, since I knew I enjoyed analyzing and solving complex problems. Although I do not have any direct sales experience, I can point to several activities that have provided valuable and relevant experience,

• During my internship, I researched market trends and customer segments for two therapeutic areas for which Kennilworth markets products and can thus 'hit the ground running' if placed on sales teams responsible for those products

• Teamed seamlessly with two groups in the marketing department, providing additional support to Product Management during the launch of a major new product

• As a double major (biology and business administration), I have the foundation to understand the scientific basis behind the products and the economic challenges facing physicians

Today's environment requires flexible, adaptable thinkers, who must understand customers' needs for both safety and economy. Having a broad academic foundation and a penchant for collaboration, I am confident I can help your group achieve its sales and marketing goals.

Ms, Parker, thank you for considering my resume. I look forward to the opportunity to meet with you in a face-to-face interview. I am eager to be an asset to Kennilworth and will do my best, if hired, to make you and other managers proud of my contributions.

Respectfully submitted,

[insert signature]

Cynthia J. Penn

Enclosure

Cover Letter Sample: Early Career with Some Sales Experience

Alan S. Foxworth
2341 Wisteria Lane
Williamsburg, VA 23185
757.253.2276 (Home) • 757.810.1490 (Mobile)

August 20, 2005

Mr. Burton C. Hasselbach
District Manager
Ethical Global Pharmaceuticals, Inc.
550 Totten Pond Road
Waltham, MA 02154

Dear Mr. Hasselbach,

I am happy to respond to your August 18, 2005 job posting in the Washington Post for a pharmaceutical sales representative. In researching the pharmaceutical industry, I noted Ethical Global's leadership position in research and development and in making its products available to underprivileged populations. Having decided to develop a career in biopharmaceutical sales and marketing, I am excited about the prospect of making a contribution to Ethical Global's worldwide sales force, and am attaching a resume for your review.

In several years of professional sales experience, I can list these achievements, which highlight my selling and leadership skills:

• Earned designation as top performer in my region for four consecutive quarters

• Received several letters of commendation from new customers (see my brag book) for excellent customer service

• Assisted in the training of new-hires in the sales organization and contributed to the update of the selling skills module of the training program

In the current tough marketing environment, I understand how essential it is to master the art of selling products while providing sustained, exceptional customer service, which exceeds client expectations. I am eager to learn the product knowledge essential to presenting pharmaceutical products effectively to physicians. A natural 'people-person,' I look forward to meeting physicians and to representing Ethical Global's products to them.

Mr, Hasselbach, thank you in advance for reviewing my resume. I look forward to the opportunity to meet with you in a face-to-face interview, where you can assess first-hand the qualities of excellence and leadership I hope to bring to your organization.

Kind Regards,

[insert signature]

Alan S. Foxworth

Enclosure

Visit Vault at **www.vault.com** for insider company profiles, expert advice, career message boards, expert resume reviews, the Vault Job Board and more.

VAULT CAREER LIBRARY   99

Brag Book

If you are not familiar with the concept of a "brag book," it is a useful tool to help interviewers get a quick look at your achievements and how former superiors have evaluated your performance.

Brag books include records of sales achievements (e.g., sales volume, market share, profit margin, etc.), letters of recommendation, awards, licenses, certificates or other evidence of continuing education, letters of praise from in-house personnel or citations for excellence on the job during previous employment, and examples of other activities (e.g., community involvement) that demonstrate leadership potential. Also include a copy of your college transcript and a record of your driving history. It is especially important to have a clean driving record, as sales reps spend a lot of time behind a company-provided wheel.

Hiring Process and Interviews

CHAPTER 8

Getting Started

There is no single over-arching formula for landing a job. Conventional wisdom is that networking or finding opportunities through contacts is the most effective way to land a position. This depends on how you handle other factors, such as technology, career objective, and target-setting.

Here's how hiring happened for one pharma sales rep. "I saw an ad in a newspaper and faxed my resume, then got hired in a week. I had two interviews. I got a call from a manager, then went in for an interview. Then, I got a call back from that manager and a second manager to come in for a second interview, which they conducted together. Typically, two people act as interviewers. The second manager hired me." Another rep provides this insight: "If you know someone, they can submit your name, but today, you still have to go through the web site."

What you do need is, first and foremost, exposure. This means people have to be able to find you—on Internet job boards, via headhunters, on corporate career web sites, and in-person via friends, associates, and other job hunters. There are some fine programs that post your resume on multiple sites, or you can do that yourself. It need not take a lot of time, as long as you have a presence out there.

The second thing you need is focus. Your resume and other materials need to be geared toward a specific industry, function and job. With so much happening online, even in-house recruiters initially screen resumes using specialized database programs, which list only resumes having certain key words or phrases. Therefore, if your resume does not contain these, you're not likely to get to first base. If you are not sure what job you want, be sure to think through what industry you wish to enter and zero in on one or two related functional areas (e.g., marketing and training, finance and accounting).

Getting past first base means ensuring your resume stays in the "in" file after being initially screened. To pass that screening, your resume must fulfill three expectations: first, it has to look perfect; second, it has to summarize your skill set clearly, and third, it has to be free of 'red flags' (e.g., employment gaps, inaccuracies in content, extremely high-level sounding

Visit Vault at **www.vault.com** for insider company profiles, expert advice, career message boards, expert resume reviews, the Vault Job Board and more.

VAULT CAREER LIBRARY   101

positions that create the impression your current application will be a step down, etc.).

The last thing you need is statistics-savvy. Be realistic about the level of effort needed to mount a successful job search within a three- to five-month period. Work backwards if you want at least two (three if the demand is strong) offers to choose from. With a 20% response, you'll need to interview at 10 companies. In order to achieve that yield of interviews, you would have to approach between 100 and 200 companies, expecting between 5 to 10% initial response rate.

That brings us back to number one, or exposure. Let technology do part of that work. Once your resume is posted on both job boards and company sites, you can then focus on the more time-intensive effort of networking. Remember that in-house recruiters need to find candidates. If they find your resume online, that does not, however, necessarily translate into a job, since hiring managers still need to make the final decision. But you may become a candidate again in the future if you are not selected for the current position.

Contacts are everywhere around you. Ever notice while in the waiting room of your doctor's office people walking in dragging a mini-suitcase and dressed to the nines? That would be a pharmaceutical sales rep in the regulation dark business suit (they really stand out in a medical environment) carrying bundles of samples and product literature. You can discreetly approach her and inquire whether you can ask her a few questions about her job. Most may not have time immediately, but might be willing to set up a time later on. Presto! You have access to a working professional who can talk about the reality of a sales job. Questioning nurses, the physician himself, or even pharmacists at one of the large drug store chains can also provide insights on how they interact with pharmaceutical industry staff.

Academic centers, especially those in major centers of research are excellent sources of referrals. Many universities make a concerted effort to help students enter the industry. Professors sometimes have their own sources of contacts via collaborative industry-academia research projects. Even career services centers have books on specific companies and schedules on when recruiters are coming to campus.

The public library also contains substantial resources. Find out which branch specializes in business topics and spend time looking over available resources. Large libraries in the center of big cities offer the most comprehensive resources. Get a card from that central library and do most of your research online. Other cool tools are uber-search engines like Factiva (a Dow Jones resource), which will give you comprehensive access to specific information needs. For example, if you ask which companies have products in Phase III clinical trials, the resulting list will tell you which companies are planning product launches, and will therefore be gearing up their sales and marketing activities.

We need to say a word or two here about contract sales organizations. These are companies dedicated to providing sales staff support to big pharmaceutical clients on a contractual basis. In recent years, some Big Pharma companies have done their sales force hiring directly from contract sales organizations. The rationale is that they are getting experienced reps who have already self-selected into the job and have already developed their selling abilities. This is not particularly good news for a college grad who has targeted the same group of potential employers, but it does give you an idea of the nature of the competition. Don't be daunted. You might try targeting one of those contract companies to cut your teeth before moving on to a full-fledged company.

Preparing for the Interview

The comprehensive list below will help you manage the run-up to your interviews. Some tasks—like obtaining a copy of your driving record—are applicable to territory sales jobs only. Still, if you are going to do any company-related driving, you should acquire a copy and keep it in your files in case you need it. Otherwise, follow the other steps below to ensure the most comprehensive preparation possible.

Research the industry, the company, and its products	
Global trends	Refer to Section I to see what is driving the industry, since all major developed market segments (the U.S., UK, EU, and Japan) have similar demographics. Emerging markets (like China and India) provide counter-currents to major trends.
National issues	Unlike other regulated markets, pricing is a big issue in the U.S. market. Besides reviewing Section I, seek other resources (public libraries have a wealth of resources, most of which are online and can be accessed from your home computer, so be sure to get a library card).

Research the industry, the company, and its products

Revenues and profits	Determine current and expected revenue and profit projections, as well as three- and five-year record
M&A	Research whether the business press has speculated on the possibility of a merger or acquisition in the next 12 months
Management	Learn of possible turnover in senior executive ranks, especially on the CEO, sales VP, or marketing VP levels
Products	Identify major products and therapeutic areas
FDA settlements	Become aware of settlements with FDA on regulatory issues, and on the consequences to the company
Litigation	Become familiar with ongoing litigation relative to specific products and assess their potential effects on the company

Document references

Academic	One or two professors
Professional	Two or three former employers, especially those in sales and marketing positions

Prepare Brag Book

Binder	Purchase a narrow three-ring binder and place documents in sheet protectors to facilitate thumbing through without damage or fumbling
Awards	Make copies of awards
Certificates	Make copies of certificates
Commendations	Make copies of employer commendations, including copies of e-mails thanking you for a job well done

Collect documents

Resume	Print copies on high-quality white or ivory paper
College transcript	Obtain from registrar to prove you have a four-year college degree from an accredited institution
Driving record	This is necessary for the sales rep position, since the company provides a car and much of the job is on the road

Prepare appearance

Suit	Clean, well-fitting suit no more than two or three years old. Be especially careful that it fits well and avoids trendy details. Safest colors are black, gray, or navy. Shirts in white or blue work best.
Accessories	Simple accessories that leave you unencumbered work best. Discreet jewelry (many say less is more here). Ensure polished shoes with matching socks or stockings.
Personal grooming	Check hair, nails, and teeth for well-groomed appearance. Avoid colognes and perfumes.
Portfolio	Purchase a black or brown one in either leather or leather-like material large enough to contain resumes, references, and other documentation

Check attitude

Deal with anxiety and fear	Being keyed-up is natural. Minimize normal jitters by practicing interview responses with a friend in a role-play situation.
Adopt a 'victory' mindset	Remind yourself of your strengths and what you bring to the job.

Visit Vault at **www.vault.com** for insider company profiles, expert advice, career message boards, expert resume reviews, the Vault Job Board and more.

VAULT CAREER LIBRARY   105

Sample Interview Questions by Position

Most companies apply variations on behavioral interviews, which seek to identify how you have responded to different situations in the past, and, by extension, how you are likely to respond once you are on the job. If you are interviewing for an entry-level job or are only a few years into your career, you are likely to be asked a series of questions about your background, and are expected not only to provide details on any aspect of your work experience but also to describe the special problems and challenges you faced and how you dealt with them. Implicit in each question is "what did you really contribute and how effectively did you cope with people issues?"

In the next section we provide a few sample questions and responses to get you thinking in the right direction. There is no absolute right answer to any given question. Be sure to role-play with a friend—or mentor—to rehearse your answers. Questions about weaknesses or inquiries about failures can be disconcerting. Remember to frame those experiences as chances to learn or to encourage greater self-knowledge.

Sample Phrases for Difficult Questions

- "I learned a great deal from that experience."

- "As a result of working on that project, I found out a lot about myself as a leader."

- "I was disappointed in my performance during that period, and resolved to improve my skills."

- "Once I understood how critical our work was going to be for the department that year, I took several steps to manage my time and attitude better."

- "As a result of the changes I made, after a few weeks, our work team was able to meet our goals despite the stress and uncertainty surrounding the impending merger."

You see the formula: Identify the problem or situation accurately, list any intervening actions, then frame your assessment of self and others in a positive way. Be particularly careful about appearing too 'perfect' or well-rehearsed, as that could be interpreted as lacking authenticity.

Entry-level pharmaceutical sales reps

Why do you want to get into pharmaceutical sales?

I enjoy working with people, and found out through several jobs that I have an aptitude for persuading and selling. The prospect of promoting products that help people feel better makes me feel good about the effort I'll be putting into the job. I know it's going to be a challenge to learn about all the products, but I look forward to that since I enjoy learning. I've got a goal-directed, competitive impulse and am fairly meticulous in keeping records. I think these qualities can be well-applied to marketing healthcare products.

Why did you select our company to apply for a sales rep position?

I became interested in your company as a result of several factors. I was impressed when the CEO directly addressed a problem that came up with the clinical trial results of a promising drug a few months ago. She set a tone of leadership and integrity for the whole company. Second, the company is one of the leaders in R&D in several major cancers and has several drugs that have extended the lifespan of cancer patients as well as improved the quality of their lives. Finally, I learned from interacting with sales reps during a preceptorship that the company provides a lot of support for its reps, which is critical when the business environment becomes challenging.

What do you believe are likely to be the greatest challenges you'll face as a pharmaceutical sales rep?

Getting access to physicians and making the case for the products I'll be responsible for within the few minutes of available face time with the physician are probably the two biggest challenges. I understand that there are creative ways of getting around these issues—by having doctors listen to presentations online, then following up with them. Even if that is possible, it's going to be critical to refine my own presentation so that I make full use of the time that is available.

How would you describe your key strengths and weaknesses?

One key strength is that I can switch gears easily and go from working independently to working as a team member in a collaborative environment. Working with people can be fun, but it does add a new dimension and requires that the team members divide the work fairly. Also, I have a strong goal-orientation, which keeps me motivated to meet the goal I've set.

How would you describe your weaknesses?

I do have a perfectionistic streak, which sometimes leads me to spend a lot of extra time making sure reports are as good as I can make them. In order to not lose perspective, I keep a list of priorities and stay time-conscious so that I don't miss deadlines. I'm also an optimist, which is basically good, but sometimes requires that I think through very carefully how much I can take on.

What do you look for in a manager?

I've had several managers during the various jobs I've had in college. Probably the most important thing is that a manager be fair, communicate performance expectations clearly, and give regular constructive feedback. One thing about selling, though, is that the job itself requires a fairly independent person to be able to do it on a daily basis.

Sales managers

Tell me about how you would manage a co-promotion arrangement in which the company's sales force is charged with marketing a product developed by the partner company, which does not itself have its own marketing capability.

That scenario is becoming increasingly common in recent years, with smaller biotechs doing most of the discovery and pre-clinical trial work on protein-type products. In those cases, the biotech management has a great deal at stake in guarding its intellectual property and needs the marketing partner— in the form of its sales force—to represent as accurately as possible the product they have developed. In these cases, we would be sure to pick only experienced sales reps, preferably with some specialized education in the technology through which the product was made (e.g., monoclonal antibodies). In addition, I would put into place a medical liaison officer to handle the most scientific questions from physicians. Finally, both parties need to set reasonable sales goals to ensure that expectations for revenue and profits are consistent with the status of the market in the product's therapeutic area.

How have you handled marketplace changes in your geographic area at your previous position?

We follow demographic shifts using several sources of data. First and foremost, we get data from our field reps, which includes notes from customers (both physicians and pharmacists). Second, our marketing department generates research through surveys and census data to pinpoint the exact nature of the changes going on in a region. In addition to that, I make sure I myself stay on top of things by monitoring state government sites, large metropolitan area newspapers, and the like. The important thing is to look at all these strands and weave them together into a coherent story of how the marketplace is changing. To do that, I meet regularly with both field reps and marketing people to share insights and confirm conclusions.

Sales trainers

Why would you like to move into the training area?

I've been attracted to teaching throughout my higher education. As both an undergraduate and graduate student, I had teaching assistantships and fellowships. Although most graduate students receive fellowships, I had already gotten experience as an undergrad. I love to learn and to help other people learn. That combination has been a good fit. As a professional, becoming a sales trainer is a mark of distinction—it says that I'm one of the best and can be trusted to represent the company with new hires. These last few years, I've earned that distinction through the several awards you see in my brag book.

How would you modify your teaching approach when marketing biotech products?

The interesting thing about marketing many biotech products is that, because their targeted patient populations are usually small and the disease condition pretty complex, the sales rep has to make a few adjustments. First, specialty reps need to understand the science, often a cancer of one sort or another, well enough to become articulate with the physician. That can be a tall order. Second, the rep fulfills an even more consultative role than usual, sometimes having to field questions about how the company's drug will affect a specific subset of patients. This means that the rep will have to be conversant in a host of possible adverse effects. To develop this level of expertise, I would suggest role plays and train to respond to different adverse effects scenarios. The ultimate goal is to have the reps speak the language of the field as fluidly as possible.

Visit Vault at **www.vault.com** for insider company profiles, expert advice, career message boards, expert resume reviews, the Vault Job Board and more.

VAULT CAREER LIBRARY   **109**

Managed markets account managers

How would you balance the issues of accessibility of drugs with the company's need to recoup its development costs?

Achieving that balance is an ongoing challenge, especially in a business environment where pricing is under relentless pressure. Accessibility is achieved by getting the product accepted in the formularies of major HMOs. But the company recoups its costs by having account managers negotiate the best price with the HMO management. How long a product gets accepted onto a formulary after it enters the marketplace is a key factor for both sides of the equation. When the company needs the high price (right after market launch) to recoup costs, the product has not yet been accepted into most formularies. That changes after a period of time, sometimes a year or more. Formulary acceptance means that the product falls under the three-tier co-pay pricing structure of most HMOs, making the drug more accessible.

Product managers

How would you assess the current business environment with respect to the launching of new products?

There's no question that marketing pharmaceuticals has become harder in recent years, mostly because of persistent downward pressure on prices and tighter regulations. That means achieving the profit margins seen in the 1990s is probably increasingly optimistic. The good news is that pharmaceutical products are fast becoming the first line of defense in the treatment of many disease conditions. Hence, the annual sales volume of products will likely continue to increase. That ultimately leads to larger markets.

One thorny issue is that globalization of the industry has highlighted the extent of uneven regulations across overseas markets. That leads to greater transaction costs and overall inefficiencies. The sourcing of later-stage steps in drug testing in foreign markets will continue to draw fire, but cost differentials and skilled labor overseas will likely keep the debate going for the near future.

Advertising specialists

Tell me how you would present a new drug to physicians, given the problems incurred in promoting pharmaceuticals in recent years.

Advertising specialists need to present products in engaging ways and provide information on the mechanism of action, the patient group for which the product has been developed, its major and minor adverse reactions, and any groups who should not be taking the drug. The piece—whether it's print advertising or a direct-to-consumer ad on TV—should have a balance between education and branding.

Market analysts

How you would use a program like SPSS in developing market analytics?

SPSS is one of the leading statistical analysis software programs and is a powerful tool for gaining insights into customers and patients. It can segment groups of patients into rational categories; for example, patients in different age groups can be understood as being in different risk categories, with, typically, older patients being in the higher risk categories and younger patients in lower risk groups.

Customer call center representatives

How would you handle a call from a patient who has been on a new drug for a few weeks and complains of vague but persistent adverse effects?

The most important thing from a customer relations perspective is to show empathy, since this patient is not feeling well. Something as simple as saying, "I'm really sorry you're not feeling well" helps the person understand that the company (through my words and attitude) cares about her and her experience. Next, I'd need to get personal information—name, age, her disease condition, her physician's name and the name of the clinic where she was treated.

After listening and capturing her story on my computer, I'd give her information on the product's adverse effects, find out what communication has occurred with her physician, and encourage her to report all symptoms. I would not try to get between her and her doctor or dispense advice on my own, and would emphasize to her that doing so would be inappropriate.

Visit Vault at www.vault.com for insider company profiles, expert advice, career message boards, expert resume reviews, the Vault Job Board and more.

VAULT CAREER LIBRARY   111

e-Business analysts

Our goal is to increase our e-business marketing by at least 25% annually over the next five years. Tell me how you would use your technical skills to help accomplish this business goal.

The internet is definitely an evolving market channel. One of the first areas to look at is how easy it is to complete transactions online. That would require getting feedback from pharmacies ordering our products in bulk to see how e-commerce transactions can be facilitated. Second, we can review and strengthen telephone support for online transactions, since customers with queries often prefer to make them by phone. Finally, I'd work with the marketing department to promote online transactions to our customers as faster and more efficient than conventional methods. Sometimes, people need a little encouragement to try a new way of doing things.

Strategic planners

Most companies launch products simultaneously in different markets. Describe some of the challenges inherent in this approach and how you might deal with them.

In recent years, simultaneous launches have become the norm, and that puts tremendous pressure on marketing teams. Several challenges arise. First, all groups have to have a consistent message—what the product is, how it's positioned, how it should be used, etc. The key to that all-important consistency is communication. Whereas the core message can be crafted from the center, groups around the world will likely want to localize their messages to achieve maximum relevancy. Second, the product needs to adhere to FDA regulations, even if it is being marketed internationally. This becomes significant when local and regional regulatory bodies do not provide as much protection as the U.S. agency. Third, product teams (the cross-functional group of professionals in charge of seeing the product to market) need to operate with optimum effectiveness. Web-based meetings, videoconferencing, and other tools help maintain a high level of interaction, so that issues are resolved quickly and decision-making is facilitated.

Questions to Ask the Interviewer

Even if you feel you are in the hot-seat, interviewing is really a two-way street. After answering questions, the interviewer will ask you if you have any of your own. This is the time to clarify any issues your research has not answered. Your goal is two-fold: first, you want to be sure you understand what you will be held responsible for in the job for which you are interviewing, and second, you want to see if the organization into which you would be entering is the one you thought it was when viewed from the outside looking in.

This second issue is particularly important, since internal turmoil within the management is usually not visible on the outside. For example, if a merger is pending, middle managers may be feeling insecure about their jobs, and hence have a defensive attitude. Alternatively, if feeling under pressure to contain costs, the much-touted training programs used to lure young new hires may be cut back until a new structure emerges and funding becomes more certain. Use this time to smoke out any red flags. If things go well, and they call you back, ask to talk to a few people in your peer group. Many companies are so gun-shy in full-time hiring these days that they schedule a second and even third round of interviews with various members of the work area to gauge how well you "fit in the company culture."

Questions about the job itself

- What therapeutic area and product line am I interviewing for?

- What are the major customer groups, patient groups, and advocacy groups in this product area?

- What is the average number of products a sales rep is typically responsible for promoting?

- How does collaboration happen in the District? Will I be team-selling or working mostly alone?

- What are the critical success factors in a pharma sales rep job?

Questions about the organization

- How is performance evaluation and feedback structured?

- What is the company's attitude toward promoting from within versus hiring managers from outside?

Visit Vault at **www.vault.com** for insider company profiles, expert advice,
career message boards, expert resume reviews, the Vault Job Board and more.

V∕\ULT CAREER LIBRARY   **113**

• Have there been any significant changes in the responsibilities of the sales force in the last 12 to 18 months?

• Do you anticipate any major product launches in the next six to 12 months?

Following Up

Be sure to send a letter or e-mail to your interviewer within a day after the interview. Although these messages may be a bit less formal than cover letters, they should contain three elements: first, thank the interviewer for his time and attention; second, bring up a point that came up in the conversation, which you would like to reemphasize or amplify and which should demonstrate your expertise in the field; and third, close with a strong message of interest in the job and your desire to make a contribution to the company.

Unfortunately, when hiring managers turn to other candidates, and you are not included on the revised list, you may never hear back from either the interviewer or anyone else. This is not to say that this practice is the rule. Many companies eventually get around to having someone in the human resources department send an e-mail informing you that you didn't make the cut. In those cases, you will at least get closure, albeit via a form letter.

Informal research among job hunters, however, suggests that the 'silent treatment' is given out more often than not. This is, at best, a crummy practice. You'll have to take the initiative—either by calling or sending an e-mail. Your message should be devoid of annoyance or defensiveness and be inquiring as to whether they found someone else with a 'better fit' or if instead something else worked against you. It is safe to frame the message in terms of "I'd like your feedback on the interview and my application since I want to learn how I can improve my presentation in future interviews."

Career Transitions

CHAPTER 9

Moving into Pharmaceutical Sales

In recent years, it has become possible to transition from an established career in a related field into positions promoting pharmaceutical products. This is a relatively new development, an outcome of companies needing quick access to sales forces with substantial scientific training. This need has in turn created opportunities for several classes of workers in scientific and healthcare occupations. In all the cases below, the movement is from the outside in. Once established in a pharma sales position, the industry offers many opportunities to move out of field sales into related career tracks (see Section III). Whatever the direction of the transition, however, in the current cost-sensitive business environment, it is essential that career changers be proactive in minimizing the actual risk—as well as the perception of risk—to the hiring company. This means being proactive in two basic ways.

First, ensure that paper credentials (resume, cover letter, brag book, etc.) clearly highlight transferable skills, aptitudes, and core competencies that will push your resume through the initial computer screening for the right skill set and secondary screening by an in-house recruiter. Specifically list those skills and competencies using the key terms summarized earlier, reinforcing them in each bullet point of specific experience.

Second, a recruiter should be able to see evidence of interest in field sales and marketing throughout the resume, cover letter, and brag book. This can mean everything from taking specialized courses or obtaining certificates to documenting excellence in customer service or persuading management to adopt a new project (remember how important persuasion and influencing skills are in modern sales methods). Finally, if you are intent on moving into a sales position and don't have any direct experience of any kind, then at minimum, obtaining knowledge of the sales process (i.e., how to begin a call, make a presentation, deal with issues and objections, and close the call) will give you an intellectual foundation on which the company can build with customized training programs.

Case 1: Nurse to Pharmaceutical Sales Representative

Nurses provide an attractive pool of medically trained workers with a keen sense of a pharmaceutical company's end user's (the patient) needs. They administer the industry products, listen to patient responses on adverse effects, and relay that information to the prescribing physician. Nurses understand treatment protocols and provide an additional vehicle for explaining how a drug works to the patient and the patient's family. This makes them particularly good candidates to promote the industry's products, especially in medical conditions, such as cancer, where ongoing, long-term treatment is likely.

The transition is relatively straightforward, with no extra education usually required. A registered nurse already has the required four-year college degree, the nursing certification, and years of hospital floor experience. That is a strong and broad foundation for an entry-level pharmaceutical sales position.

Transition strategy

The easiest transition is to identify a company producing the drug(s) that a nurse has used in primary care. For example, an oncology nurse who has administered major cancer-fighting drugs, such as taxol and carboplatin, might consider moving to a company that specializes in oncology drugs. That will give her a substantial lead in product knowledge relative to other entry-level reps, and may likely result in a more senior status at entry.

The most important issue will then be the nurse's selling skills—or lack thereof. Supposing that potential has been clearly demonstrated in paper credentials and the nurse has already taken a selling skills seminar, it remains only to demonstrate an actual selling encounter. Role play works well here. Find a friend or mentor to take on the role of interviewer and practice a sales pitch for a pharmaceutical product, pretending the interviewer is a physician, pharmacist, or hospital formulary manager. Practice until you feel completely comfortable. It is not unlikely that the interviewer will ask you to promote other products, including familiar consumer products—everything from aspirin to water bottles—just to gauge how intellectually agile and poised you are.

Case 2: BS-level Associate Scientist to Pharmaceutical Sales Rep

Let's say you graduated from college a couple of years ago and elected to spend a few years in industry before moving on to graduate school. You found a job as an associate scientist at a biotech company, which has been growing its scientific staff but does not yet have a product on the market. You love the entrepreneurial spirit that is driving the company's founders, you're paid well, and enjoy the collegial atmosphere among your colleagues. But the bench work that seemed so interesting during those first six months on the job now seems repetitive, uncreative, and, well, just plain dull. You feel restless and want to get a better sense of what's happening.

Worse, you realize that those nagging doubts you had about getting a doctorate and heading for a research career have matured to a full-fledged "No, that's not what I want to do with my life." Where your peers see meetings as a waste of time, you jump at the chance to get together with people in other groups to coordinate schedules and iron out other inevitable stresses that arise from a brisk growth rate. "I'm a people person," you say. "I want to make decisions that have a more direct impact on people and on the company itself," Ok. It happens all the time.

Transition strategy

From that position, many people decide to go on to graduate business programs, earn an MBA and then apply for a sales or marketing position. That is a very viable strategy, as you have the scientific foundation, a few years of industry experience, and a business education foundation from which to build upon. If you opt for a full-time MBA program, an internship between the first and second year will give you an entrée into a company.

But suppose you're not quite ready to hit the books again or you would prefer to have more industry experience before investing in a management program. After all, management is not the only alternative to bench research. You take a few self-assessments and find out what you have always known—that you are comfortable working with people. You research the industry and find out that two-thirds of the drugs in development are biotech drugs. You network and get informational interviews with people who work with Big Pharma companies to co-promote biotech drugs developed by small research-driven firms like yours. Finally, you conclude that you would like to spend your days in the same professional sandbox as those obliging people who gave you a sneak peak at their side of the house. That's a lot good work done. You have clarity of purpose. You have a goal.

Because you are reading this and can easily flip back to the nurse's case, you decide on getting selling skills training, including the seminar and role play. But without clinical experience, you have to be resourceful. Hanging out at the doctor's office (to catch up on that physical, flu shot, cholesterol check, whatever), you strike up a conversation with several sales reps waiting to see the doctor. One of them agrees to take you on a field preceptorship for a week. This means riding along all day with the rep, watching him prepare for calls, make them, do follow up, fit in online training, and do ancillary work. Over a week's time, the schedule and pacing of a rep's work life becomes apparent and you become familiar with every aspect of her responsibilities. The preceptorship should figure prominently in your resume and cover letter and emphasize that nitty-gritty understanding of the job. The same goes for that selling skills seminar.

Creating a list of target companies is the next step. Find companies who market products using similar technology as those you've become familiar with on the job. For example, if you've worked making monoclonal antibodies, then companies marketing drugs using a similar method would find your background attractive. It is not, however, necessary to be too specialized at this stage. You are likely to be as attractive as a specialty rep of any number of biotech products as to a Big Pharma company co-promoting a product with a biotech company. Alternatively, you might consider becoming a specialty rep at a Big Biotech company, the top 10 of which hold as much as 85% of the industry's revenues.

A final note to young scientists: do not underestimate the importance of presenting a consistently polished appearance, and not just for the interview. The way you present yourself during the interview is the same as how you are expected to dress day to day.

Case 3: Healthcare Analyst to Pharmaceutical Sales Rep

Like the associate scientist, you landed a job as an assistant healthcare analyst out of college and after three or four years have been promoted to associate healthcare analyst. Your days have been packed with information gathering, number crunching for the senior analyst, researching different companies to determine their disposition toward either purchase or sale, and analysis,

analysis, analysis. Your life is about getting data, figuring out what it means, and sending it up the line for decision makers to turn into recommendations for key clients. You never actually meet with those clients or, for that matter, with the senior analyst. In fact, most of your days are spent in a small cubicle surrounded by flat screens, inboxes, and just enough free desk space to accommodate a coffee mug, keyboard and notebook. The latter is for analog writing, still necessary in our not-yet-fully-digitized world. Do you feel hemmed in? Restless and isolated? Can't beat the pay. Benefits include full coverage for health and dental insurance. Yet you wonder, is this all there is?

Fortunately, you are reading this text and decide to take your cue from the nurse and scientist. But you feel you have more business savvy than either of them and don't see why you can't move into a marketing position. Meticulous by nature, you take personal assessments and network to create contacts. Unlike the scientist, you use your familiarity with the industry to identify product managers at a couple of companies you might be interesting in targeting. One actually responds to your request for an informational interview. You also track down the Web sites for trade associations and find places like bio.org and Phrma.com, make direct contact with them, and land two more contacts for informational interviews. One is with a sales manager; the other with a market development manager. Excited, you go through the interviews only to be told virtually the same thing by all three; If you want to be a professional marketer of biopharmaceuticals, there is no better place to begin your career than in a field sales position. There, over a year or two, you see what it really takes to bring in revenues. Companies expect people to move on (see Section III), but consider field sales an excellent foundation for marketing jobs later on.

Transition strategy

From inside that cubicle, you might feel just as odd as your prospective colleagues at the bench or the hospital floor. You are leaving a peer group that is comfortable for a space where you are not. But armed with the work you've done so far, you take an all-of-the-above approach: you do the selling skills seminar, enlist a friend to role-play with, and get a field preceptorship using the sales contact. From your interviews, you understand that marketing positions require MBAs, but decide you'd rather embark on a program with a company sponsorship so as not to disrupt your career.

Your stellar academic record and analytical professional experience provide a strong foundation and makes you an attractive candidate to an in-house recruiter. The challenge is to demonstrate your "people skills," i.e., your ability to collaborate with others, to work in a team-oriented environment, and to meet those all-important sales targets week after week and month after month. You already know this, so you can anticipate and prepare. Your paper credentials demonstrate instances where your inter-personal skills ameliorated a situation on the job or maintained a forward momentum where friction among colleagues might have threatened meeting a target.

Also consider outside activities that illustrate influence, persuasion, and collaboration skills, such as contributions to your faith organization or favorite charity. If you've been too busy, consider offering your time and energy on a project that can demonstrate your inherent aptitudes in these areas. If the museum in your city is putting on a fall gala to raise money for a program to bring art to impoverished children and you decide to volunteer assisting the organizing committee, you can feel comfortable about having made a legitimate contribution that can be assessed by a letter from the event chairperson. The important thing is to identify projects and organization where you can make a genuine contribution that permits your natural aptitudes to shine.

Tips on Career Transitions

There is no absolute right or wrong way to go about a career transition. The choice of more formal schooling is a double-edged sword. Unless you are very clear on your goals, the sheer intensity and competitiveness of a full-time program, let alone the expense and disruption to your earning power, is bound to create its own stresses. Happily, many advanced program institutions, such as business schools, are increasingly offering online and certificate programs, which enable you to sample a new field with a limited investment in time, energy, and money.

It is essential that you obtain first-hand information and insights from people actually doing the work you think you want to do. Whatever the effort, be purposeful in pursuing informational interviews, knowing that once the ice is broken, most people love to talk about their work. Be sure to follow up each interview with a prompt thank-you note for the person's time and attention. Most people e-mail such notes these days, but if you send one handwritten by snail mail, it will be even more appreciated — and remembered — since few people take the time to prepare them that way.

Finally, directly related experience is the ultimate curtailer of risk. If you want to sell and are coming from a background that suggests you may not have a good personality fit, facilitate the hiring manager's decision by proving you've not only already learned both the theory and process of selling but you actually took on a project or position where you had to actually do it. Ultimately, your path to confidence and fun in your job is your own. Create it with your own integrity.

Visit Vault at **www.vault.com** for insider company profiles, expert advice, career message boards, expert resume reviews, the Vault Job Board and more.

VAULT CAREER LIBRARY 121

Career Paths

CHAPTER 10

Career Development: Leadership Programs, Mentors

The biopharmaceutical industry offers a wealth of opportunities for career development, with more tools available within the larger, fully integrated companies. Most large and many mid-size companies offer several or all of the tools discussed below. You may also want to use different methods at different times in your career. For example, if you are sure you like sales, you may want to work for promotions in the sales function before applying for a leadership program. Alternatively, you may want to establish yourself in your area before requesting either a rotation or a flexible work option.

Leadership and management development programs

Most large companies have programs aimed at developing promising employees and moving them to management positions. They are typically called leadership development or management development programs and are essentially intensive, long-term, in-house training programs. Getting accepted is usually highly competitive, as these programs carry a lot of prestige inside the corporation. Management development programs usually consist of classroom work, special projects, assessment tools, coaching, and testing.

Mentors

Mentors can offer special attention and faster insight into the company and industry. Some companies have formal programs for people accepted into management development programs. In many instances, managers can serve in a mentoring capacity, especially during evaluation periods, where they can affirm your strengths, help you understand your weaknesses, and work with you to devise professional development plans to address them.

Rotations

Rotations are organized, time-limited periods of exposure to different areas of activity that will give you more experience and help you understand where you will make the greatest contribution. Rotations can be in training, field support, HR, sales administration, or any of the marketing support areas (i.e., advertising and promotion, e-business, marketing strategy, etc.) Typically lasting from three months to two years, many rotations also require working at a different site. For example, field reps can do a training rotation at the home office.

Flexible work hours

Flexible work hours are becoming an increasingly significant factor in career development, since many employees (especially women) choose to have families after some years in the workforce. In the last one or two decades, corporations have come to understand the cost of losing good employees in whom they had already invested time and training. Job-sharing and part-time work have become available in many companies as a solution to this problem. That's the good news.

The not-so-good news is that exercising these options may have various impacts on your career development. Just because the company makes "flexibility" available does not mean that it is universally accepted. The company culture is key here. If you are considering this option when you expect to have a family, check discreetly on how flex-work has worked for the people (read, women, in most cases) who have opted in. How long were they on flex or part-time hours? When did they go back to full-time status? How did that period impact their status in the organization? Are there women in senior management positions who have taken a similar path? The earlier you know the answers to these questions, the better. Ideally, you would find out before joining a company, but that may not be possible. Once inside, inquire informally, seeking people who are likely to speak to you frankly. Corporations are, by and large, still on the learning curve in establishing a framework where people (read, both mothers and fathers) can be both good employees and good parents.

Career Path Cases

Once you are hired, chances are you will have your hands full doing the job. There will also be managers supervising your progress. Ideally, they will function as mentors as well, helping you clarify where you'd like to move toward after you've established yourself. Going into a job, however, it's smarter to have some idea—especially in the fast-moving and competitive sales and marketing function—of what you'd like to see on the other side.

Here are actual careers of people currently inside the industry, which can serve as models for you. Although each company's titles will be a little different, the types of entry points, actual positions, and possible future steps are consistent throughout the industry.

Field sales

In addition to incentive compensation, most companies also have carefully defined promotion criteria. These tend to be quite similar across the industry, though you can expect individual companies to word those criteria a little differently as well as wish to keep their standards confidential. This is due more to the highly competitive nature of pharmaceutical sales, especially in those product groups that are mass-marketed (and hence generate mass profits), than to any mysterious expectations.

To be promoted, field reps should generate revenues at least in the upper half of their peer group and meet a host of other specific performance criteria, such as maintaining customer satisfaction, arranging for relevant and informative educational events for physician customers, and optimizing face-to-face contact with physicians. Other criteria involve proficiency in managing the logistics and organizational aspects of the job.

Career Path of a Pharmaceutical Sales Representative

Since this is an entry-level position, people get in either as external hires, usually with some previous sales experience, or as experienced pharmaceutical sales representatives from other companies.

One specialty sales representative's actual career

1990—1995	Pharmaceutical sales representative
1995—2001	Specialty sales representative
2001—2004	Hospital representative
2004—Present	Senior Executive Specialty Sales Representative

The specialty sales representative's own assessment

"As for sales, I find it challenging. It's rewarding to know that you've educated the physicians on disease states and then they have prescribed our products and it's a great feeling of satisfaction knowing that we are improving the patients' quality of life. We build rapport with the physicians, nurse practitioners, nurses, and physician assistants."

Visit Vault at **www.vault.com** for insider company profiles, expert advice, career message boards, expert resume reviews, the Vault Job Board and more.

V/\ULT CAREER LIBRARY   **125**

Analysis

From field sales, this rep can move into any one of three possible tracks: first, other field sales positions like therapeutic specialist, medical group representative, and specialist account manager; second, sales management, with first-level management titles like district sales manager; and marketing support positions like regional trainer and regional analyst.

Managed markets

Moving up in managed markets requires at least six to eight years of direct experience, much of which can be obtained by working as a team member on a national account team. With many millions of dollars at stake in these corporate accounts, promotion criteria stress proven achievement in equal parts business analysis, customer management, and team management. Expertise in understanding the issues and pressures of healthcare financing is a must. Obtaining the all important agreements to include company products on a healthcare insurer's formulary is paramount, as that ensures distribution to the end user—the patient. Since most companies manage corporate accounts in teams, demonstrated team leadership ability is an important component of a promotion candidate's upward mobility.

Career Path of a Managed Markets Account Manager

Only seasoned professionals can get into managed markets, as these are typically national accounts often worth tens of millions of dollars. Sales experience is most valuable, as that provides the critical customer exposure. Sales jobs with titles such as district sales manager, therapeutic specialist manager, medical group representative, or account manager in a specialty business unit provide this experience. In addition, more recently created jobs, such as managed markets business development analyst, also provide needed context.

One managed markets account manager's actual career

1996–1998	Co-op Program, XYZ University
1998–2000	Information control administrator in pharma trade operations

2000—2001	Information analyst in contract management group
2001—2003	Manager of contract systems and information management
2003—2004	Business development manager, CIGNA national account team
2004—Present	Senior account manager

The managed markets account manager's own assessment

"I've always enjoyed working with customers. My customer is a national pharmacy benefit manager or PBM. They cover some 65 million people through 1,600 plan sponsors. Our company has six national account managers and we work in teams of two per national account."

"Managed care can have a great influence on physician prescribing habits, so it is important to be successful in gaining formulary access for our products. As an account manager, I am the primary contact for the account, so communication skills are essential. You have to network with all stakeholders for each product—field sales, marketing, upper management, contracting, and most importantly, with the customer."

Analysis

The managed markets account manager can move into several areas: first, continue in managed markets as a national account manager; second, sales positions like district sales manager, therapeutic specialist manager, or regional sales director in a specialty business unit; and third, marketing positions like regional analyst.

Sales management

Most companies require several years as a district sales manager before considering promotion to the next level in sales management. Just as in field sales, most companies have their own internal benchmarks for promotion. Sales managers need to "make their numbers" from quarter to quarter and year to year; they need to get new hires up and running quickly so that the latter generate their share of revenues for the district. The best sales managers continually develop tactics to optimize their reps' presentations to physician customers. On the administrative side, keeping a consistent watch over market trends and creating strategies for meeting those all-important sales goals set the best sales managers apart.

Visit Vault at **www.vault.com** for insider company profiles, expert advice, career message boards, expert resume reviews, the Vault Job Board and more.

VAULT CAREER LIBRARY   **127**

Career Path of a District Sales Manager

There are two possible tracks into this position: first, sales jobs with titles like pharmaceutical sales representative, specialty sales representative, account manager, specialty business unit, and managed markets account manager; and second, marketing support jobs with titles like regional trainer and regional analyst.

One district sales manager's actual career

1997–2000	Pharmaceutical sales representative
2000–2003	Hospital representative
2003–Present	District sales manager

The district sales manager's own assessment

"Our job is very meaningful—we are making a difference in people's lives. I believe the information we disseminate is so very important to the doctor who is using that information to prescribe and help sick people. To me, that's very inspirational, and it's motivating."

"I started my sales career after graduating from pharmacy school. I figured a pharmaceutical sales job was like being a proactive pharmacist. Instead of passively waiting for the script to come in and filling it, I had the opportunity to affect the doctor's decision before writing the script."

Analysis

From here, the district sales manager can move either to sales management or marketing, with sales titles like regional sales director and regional vice president and marketing titles like market development manager.

Marketing management

Most companies have several levels of positions in the product management track. At the senior level, product managers will have accumulated 8 or more years of experience, with at least four in successfully launching either new products or product line extensions. In addition to increased number of years of direct experience, moving up requires that candidates demonstrate increasing depth in all performance areas. On the analytical side, this means having proven ability to make difficult decisions in complex and rapidly changing business environments, to perform financial analysis and interpret results. On the "people" side, promotion criteria emphasize continual effective interfacing with peers in other functional areas who are not direct reports, team leadership, and development of marketing staff.

Career Path of a Product Manager

Product management is one of the most critical areas of the company, since the product manager oversees all aspects of launching a product in the marketplace and maintaining its profitability once it reaches consumers. Experience in any one of three tracks can lead to a job as a product manager: sales positions like pharmaceutical sales representative or district sales manager; marketing positions like customer response center representative or market development manager; or marketing support positions like regional trainer or regional analyst.

One product manager's actual career

1997–1999	Pharma sales representative
1999–2001	Hospital representative
2001–2002	Associate manager, sector operations
2002–2003	Associate product manager
2003–Present	Product manager

The product manager's own assessment

"I've always known I wanted to work in marketing, and I was lucky to have found the opportunity. My experience as a sales rep and in sales support has helped me become a better marketer. Sales taught me to identify customer needs and to provide a consistent message. In marketing, I create selling opportunities for the field force by providing them with materials designed to highlight our products' therapeutic value and motivate physicians to prescribe our products."

"As a product manager for a new product, I'm part of a team that's getting the chance to start from scratch, to create the whole plan, the whole campaign, the copy strategy, the operational plan, the message, everything that's going to help the field drive the business. And I think that's the most rewarding part of what I do."

Analysis

The product manager can move along two tracks: first, in marketing as a product director or market development manager; and second, in sales as an account manager for a specialty business unit, district sales manager, or regional vice president.

Visit Vault at **www.vault.com** for insider company profiles, expert advice, career message boards, expert resume reviews, the Vault Job Board and more.

VAULT CAREER LIBRARY   **129**

Marketing support: sales training

In addition to direct experience, moving up in sales training requires developing organizational and communication skills. Specifically, candidates for promotion should exhibit increasing ability to work independently and to use their own judgment both in and out of the classroom as well as the ability to manage several complex projects concurrently. On the "people" side, senior trainers develop an increasingly dynamic presentation style and more sophisticated communication skills, such as influencing and persuading. These latter skills are particularly important wherever organizational hierarchies are flattening and therefore require people to gain cooperation from others to achieve company goals.

Career Path of a Regional Trainer

Most regional trainers have had direct contact with customers and are usually selected from the ranks of pharmaceutical sales representatives. However, some may move into training from marketing support positions like customer response center representative, if they can demonstrate some previous field experience.

One regional trainer's actual career

1996 – 1999	Pharmaceutical sales representative
1999 – 2001	Senior sales representative
2001 – 2003	Executive senior sales representative
2004 – Present	Senior regional trainer

The regional trainer's own assessment

"I had sales territories in Pennsylvania and California. When changing territories, I set out to build the fundamentals — to make sure I call on the right people, with the right frequency, and the right message. You can't underestimate the importance of being motivated."

"The job of regional trainer is very rewarding, because we provide the newly hired sales representatives with the foundation they will need to succeed in their in-house training program. And I believe our field force is as successful as it is because they get excellent training. Surveys show that the force believes their training is a significant contributor to their success. That's something that provides a lot of personal and professional satisfaction."

Analysis

The regional trainer has several career choices: first, move up inside the training area; second, sales management in the district sales manager job; third, move to human resources, another area of marketing support, with titles like recruitment account manager; or fourth, move to marketing in a marketing analyst or regional analyst position.

Visit Vault at **www.vault.com** for insider company profiles, expert advice, career message boards, expert resume reviews, the Vault Job Board and more.

VAULT CAREER LIBRARY   **131**

ON THE JOB

Corporate Policies

CHAPTER 11

Compensation Plans

Most pharmaceutical sales positions are compensated on a comprehensive package of base salary plus incentives, which include bonuses, stock options, recognition awards, and other prizes.

Base salary

Field sales reps are paid on a base salary plus incentive compensation. Base salaries differ depending on geographic location, with larger, more expensive urban settings leaning toward the higher end of the range.

Bonuses

Bonuses are tied to meeting sales goals and are based on a percentage of base salary, with typical ranges between 2 and 16%, depending on individual, team, and overall territory performance. Bonuses are fairly typical of the industry and essentially function as commissions. Remember that field reps close sales by obtaining commitments from physicians—no money ever changes hands.

Stock options

Most companies offer their full-time employees stock options as part of their compensation program, knowing that many people view them as assets and a form of compensation. Much has been made, however, of the value of stock options and whether they constitute real compensation. From a strictly economic perspective, if your job performance can affect the price of the company's stock, then stock options are true compensation. If, on the other hand, you are given options in lieu of hard cash and your job is either entry-level or very far away from any impact on the stock price, then those options do not necessarily make up for all those extra hours (beyond the standard 40) of uncompensated labor.

Options can create a sense of ownership and work toward a common goal, but that was a cold comfort to high-technology employees whose options went "under water" (worth less than the price at which they were issued) after the tech meltdown a few years ago. Nonetheless, unless you work for a very small biotech, whose technology is unproven and whose stock is therefore likely to be volatile, you should accept those options graciously if offered.

Profit-sharing

Profit sharing is made at the discretion of senior management when the company exceeds its profit expectations. Management sets aside a set number of dollars from total profits to distribute among employees. This is usually a great motivator and gives employees a sense of ownership in the success of the enterprise as a whole.

Recognition Awards and Other Prizes

Beyond monetary compensation, most companies have additional ways of making you feel good about your achievements. Recognition awards, such as plaques or certificates specifying specific achievements, provide visibility and peer respect. These become especially important when the company is going through a rough spell or the economy is on a downturn and money is tight.

Many companies offer still other prizes for meeting and exceeding sales goals. Vacations with spouse allowances at coveted locations (e.g., Hawaii) over and above regular vacation time can entice people to stay out there and promote the company's products.

Benefits

Pharmaceutical companies have traditionally had the most comprehensive set of benefits of any American industry, with the larger companies having a broader scope and the smaller ones a relatively more limited scope.

Health and dental insurance

Most pharmaceutical companies have a full complement of medical and dental insurance. Depending on the size, age, and economic health of the company, employees are expected to pick up a portion of the monthly premiums. Traditionally, Big Pharma companies have been the most generous in picking up most, if not all, of the health insurance tab, but that expectation may not hold out, as more companies feel the impact of competing generics and other market factors. You can, however, expect a menu of options to choose from, depending on your personal and family needs.

It is also likely that Health Savings Accounts (HSAs) will be made increasingly available to employees, as a way to lower monthly premiums. Be very careful here, since lower premiums come with high deductibles. Those pushing HSAs will extol the virtues of the accounts' tax-free status and of your ownership of its assets. But HSAs shift the burden of risk from the employer and insurer to the individual. In early 2005, the "fine print" on HSAs is being constructed. Be sure to understand just how much liability the HSA plan places on you and whether you are comfortable with that risk level. Also, inquire about the backup insurance provided once that high deductible is reached. Finally, take an honest look at your health status and determine if you are at risk of a chronic disease if you are overweight, a sports-related accident if you are athletic, or if you have a family history that puts you in a high-risk category.

Life and disability insurance

Most companies offer several types of life insurance as well as comprehensive disability insurance, often at no cost to employees. If you have a family, check on the extent of life insurance, as you may want additional coverage. This will largely depend on your age, number of dependents, and whether your spouse provides a second income. Most people pay little attention to disability insurance, until something happens and they need it. Unless you are exposed to hazardous chemicals, the most significant risk posed by professional jobs is the long-term, chronic but low stress of long hours sitting behind the wheel or writing on laptops in odd positions.

Retirement plans

Retirement plans come in two basic types: defined benefit and defined contribution. Traditionally, corporations have had defined benefit plans, wherein the company pledges a specific retirement benefit based on the number of years of service of an employee. Defined benefit plans typically also have a vesting requirement, i.e., the company contribution becomes fully available only after a specific number of years of service. This stipulation helped ensure employees would choose to stay inside the system rather than job hop to other, potentially competing firms. Defined benefit plans place

Visit Vault at **www.vault.com** for insider company profiles, expert advice, career message boards, expert resume reviews, the Vault Job Board and more.

VAULT CAREER LIBRARY   **137**

long-term liabilities on companies, in the form of pension payments to former employees. In time, many boards of directors decided that the competitive environment made such a structure too expensive to sustain.

In the last 15 to 20 years, corporations have gradually shifted to defined contributions plans, most commonly known as 401(k) Plans. Here, the company's contribution to an employee's retirement plan is paid up front, and often is fully available, without vesting requirements. Employees may choose of a handful of investment options, typically professionally managed mutual funds (i.e., equity, equity-income, income, or cash funds). Employees may shift their assets among available funds and even take out loans against their funds, within specified constraints. By paying up front, the company removes future pension liabilities from its books. That reduces uncertainty for the corporation, and puts the onus of managing retirement funds on the employee and the funds' managers.

Because pharmaceuticals is a traditional industry, some companies may have elements of both types of plans, with older workers tied to defined benefit plans and younger workers to defined contribution plans. The trend is moving relentlessly toward the latter.

Car allowance

Pharmaceutical companies provide their sales reps with cars for both professional and personal use. This is really one of the biggest benefits of a Sales job. The company provides insurance and a gas allowance. The full-size cars can also be traded in for a new model after logging a certain number of miles, often as low as 50,000 miles. If that seems lavish, think about it. Would a company prefer to keep their fleets relatively new or incur maintenance-related delays that can eat up valuable face time with customers?

Remember that that car is essentially a sales rep's office. Pre-call planning and post-call notes are often completed in the car. The Rep carries drug samples, product information, files on current and prospective customers, other reference material, and personal items in the car.

Laptop computers

Most companies issue laptop computers to their sales force to maintain their reports and communicate with the company's sales support group and sales management. The laptops are usually fairly current models. Generally, corporations update their hardware technology every three years. They also maintain comprehensive support services. Identifying the name and contact information for the "computer guys" is one of the most useful actions upon getting hired. They will help you get up to speed on the specific software the company is using.

Educational reimbursement

The pharmaceutical industry is one of the most training-intensive of all industries. Most companies have generous allowances for obtaining advanced degrees while on the job. Be sure to understand what that allowance is and what conditions are attached to obtaining reimbursements. Also be sure to check how much time the company will allow you to take off to attend classes scheduled during business hours. While many companies will have an allotment, expect that most would prefer you meet those educational goals on your own time.

Travel

Field sales reps typically have a geographic territory to cover with a list of physicians and pharmacists to call upon regularly. Traveling occurs within those boundaries and is part of the field rep's daily routine. Which physician or pharmacist, how often to call, and what to present to them is carefully arranged with the home office. Sometimes, people work in teams, which means that a team of two or three shares the territory, in which case, the geographic scope of travel becomes reduced by half.

Dress Code

In most pharmaceutical sales positions, the way you dress for the interview is the way you dress for work every day. A visit to your doctor's office will confirm this statement. Pharmaceutical reps stand out for their dark, conservative, highly polished attire. This is fairly standard throughout the industry and is meant to maximize the professionalism of the field force with respect to their physician customers.

By the time someone becomes a district manager, wearing dress suits has become a habit. Where shirtsleeves may be acceptable in the office, the full suit is mandatory when dealing with customers. District managers are also

Visit Vault at **www.vault.com** for insider company profiles, expert advice,
career message boards, expert resume reviews, the Vault Job Board and more.

V/\ULT CAREER LIBRARY   **139**

role models to new sales reps, who can pick up cues on appearance and emeanor from their managers.

The formal code also applies to managed markets people, since they deal with large, corporate customers.

The dress code varies somewhat in different areas of the marketing organization. Trainers have more leeway, since they are dealing with in-house people, and many training environments do not require full dress suits. If anything, trainers need to appear accessible and friendly so as to optimize the learning environment.

Product managers may wear suits to work, but often work abandon their jackets shortly after arriving at the office. Given that they are essentially field commanders for the product, they need to have maximum comfort. It is expected that presentations and other interactions with superiors happen with the full uniform.

The rule of thumb is that when in doubt, go conservative. It is especially important to note that, in addition to fine clothing, excellent hygiene and personal grooming is expected. That may seem self-evident, but the trick is not to overdo it, i.e., no colognes or perfumes for both genders, understated accessories, and no more than five pieces of jewelry (watch, earrings, one ring, and one bracelet) for women. Industry insiders also point out the importance of clean, well polished shoes!

Socializing and Networking

Field sales reps operate from home and their mobile offices in their cars, with occasional trips to the home office for meetings. Training events have traditionally been located at pleasant venues, which offer reps plenty of time to relax and socialize with peers. Here, the informal training is just as important as the classroom work, with people sharing war stories, tips on handling contacts with physicians, and insights on how the industry and marketplace are evolving.

Field reps arrange lunchtime meetings with medical specialists to brief physicians on the latest science in their field and how the rep's products are coming along the testing process. These events are opportunities for reps to network among other professionals and to develop their familiarity and fluency in the medical science in question.

Product launches are high-energy events that provide ample opportunity to both socialize and network among the many types of in-house specialists from different functional areas required to get a product to market. For a field rep at the beginning of her career, meeting product managers, advertising and promotion managers, customer support specialists, and regional training manager is a great way to become familiar with people actually doing jobs that might be options in the future.

Contacts obtained through any of these avenues become an important part of your informal network. You can tap into them when you begin exploring your next steps.

Employee Relations

All companies have similar labor relations policies (i.e., affirmative action, non-discrimination, recruiting and hiring policies, receptivity to women and minorities, employee training and development, etc.) to ensure fairness in hiring and promotion. Employee relations officers implement these policies, usually from human resource departments. Companies take these policies seriously partly because they may be vulnerable to discrimination suits and negative publicity in the media. More importantly, with companies invested in gaining access to increasingly diverse customers, it is to their advantage to hire sales and marketing staff that bring insight into culturally diverse groups.

Visit Vault at **www.vault.com** for insider company profiles, expert advice, career message boards, expert resume reviews, the Vault Job Board and more.

V/\ULT CAREER LIBRARY   **141**

Life on the Job

Sales and marketing professional have similar lifestyles throughout the industry. In this chapter, we take a look at a cross-section of people representative of their specific functional areas.

The lifestyle of a pharmaceutical sales rep is standard throughout the industry and has been well-documented in industry publications. The two examples below include insights on the downside of this lucrative job. In addition, we profile representatives of the major career tracks discussed. When reading these pieces, imagine yourself going through the days and activities described. How clearly do you see yourself in the roles presented?

Executive Sales Representative

The sales rep profiled here promotes general therapeutic products and has been on the job long enough to have earned at least one promotion. Note the nursing degree and how, combined with communication skills, it translates into an attractive base salary. Given the continual daily personal contact, the admission of an element of loneliness in this job is noteworthy.

Name of position	Pharmaceutical Executive Sales Representative
Function	Sales
Education level	Hospital Diploma RN; BS, Communications
Company type and size	Large, public, international pharmaceuticals company
Typical number of hours per week	45-50 hours
Salary range	$60K—$120K base; bonus: based on meeting and exceeding market share goals (from $5K per quarter); bonuses are uncapped
Perks	Stock options, tied to bonus structure—top 10% will be rewarded with extra stock; each year the top 25% of sales reps are part of the Winner's Circle, get special prizes and vacations; company car and associated expenses (insurance and mileage)

Responsibilities

I am responsible for maintaining and growing the market share of my products. I'm given a list of target physicians in my territory and am expected to see 8—10 physicians per day. Through data provided by the marketing department, I know exactly what an MD is prescribing before going in to see him. I do both pre—and post-call planning. I am also expected to do business analysis—i.e., to maintain lists of market growth forms to figure out where our growth is and where our growth potential is.

I work in a team—there are two other reps on the same level I'm in. Three geographies work for the same district sales manager—that's a total of 9 reps and 1 or 2 specialty reps. I have to coordinate with teammates to determine the tactics for approaching an MD. Our team works out a routing schedule, with three-week rotations. So, for any given week, I know exactly where to go. I schedule lunches in the week where I'm going to be in that town.

I am also expected to go to two pharmacies per day—to see what they have back-ordered and what continuing education they have. I usually do a pharmacy call in the morning, since the pharmacist is not likely to be busy during that timeframe. That knocks one call out of the way. It also kind of gets your mouth in gear.

I also do a lot of continuing education, much of which happens over lunch. We usually have 2 or 3 lunches per week. We provide lunch for the entire staff, since they receive the education. Finally, we have special projects—such as arranging dinner meetings with physicians, nurses and other healthcare professionals to provide forums where specialists can talk with each other.

A typical day

7:45 a.m.	Leave home; drive to first call; do pre-call planning
8:45 a.m.-12:00 p.m.	Pharmacy visit Physician office visits
12:00 p.m.-2:00 pm	Offices closed; lunch with staff and/or physicians; great chance to talk to them; catch up on computer work; file reports. Call in specialist to—an office to talk about important issues (e.g., latest post-launch data on adverse effects or ongoing clinical results for drugs in development)

2:00 p.m.-5:00 p.m.	Pharmacy visit
	Physician office visits
5:00 p.m.-6:30 p.m.	Evening event set up; usually one per month. This involves making sure the meeting room is ready (i.e., slide projector, easel for note pad, writing implements, refreshments, etc.)
6:30 p.m.-9:00 p.m.	Host evening event. This involves introducing the speaker(s), moderating the meeting, and making a presentation of how my company's product fits into the disease state that the physician experts are discussing.
9:00 p.m.	Follow up on the computer at home to complete post-call planning (e.g., write up notes, document questions and responses, identify outstanding issues and queries, special needs, etc.)

Uppers and downers

Uppers	Downers
It's not a 9-to-5 job. It's an independent lifestyle. We all carry the same products and the same compensation, so that makes teamwork and collaboration very easy. We're very well taken care of. We stay in nice places and the bonus structure adds incentives to our work.	It can be lonely. You don't have an office to go to. It's pretty much you driving around all day. You don't have that office camaraderie except when we have big meetings, and that can be kind of weird. The people at the physician offices can become your family. Sometimes I bring Christmas party food and share it at a doctor's office. There are some physicians with whom you develop great rapport. Getting organized enough can be hard for some people. Some companies have networked computers that can keep track of when you are making your calls, so if you don't get started till late, that could become a problem. Access is difficult; a lot of physicians don't have a lot of time. Five minutes a piece and 15 reps a day can add an extra hour to the physician's day!

Visit Vault at **www.vault.com** for insider company profiles, expert advice,
career message boards, expert resume reviews, the Vault Job Board and more.

VAULT CAREER LIBRARY   **145**

Success criteria

The most important success criteria are being flexible and being able to get along with people. Don't get crushed when they say no. See it as an opportunity to work on the problem—to let the situation evolve. So good people skills is a crucial asset.

You also have to have an ability to grasp medical knowledge—to be able to talk to a doctor. If he switches gears and talks about an area outside the product's field, you have to be able to converse with him.

Being a nurse, I've learned to figure out what a physician really needs, instead of what he says he needs. You have to be perceptive, to learn to read people. I can sense when a very nice physician is tense or not in a position to talk to me. It's not about my agenda, but theirs. Then I just say, "This doesn't seem like a good time to talk. I'll be back another day and we can talk then." They're usually very appreciative and positively disposed to talk to me the next time I call on them.

Advice for jobseekers

Get sales experience, especially in consumer products. Develop an understanding of the industry and its foremost issues to show the interviewer that you understand the challenges you will be facing. Also research the job and practice your responses to anticipated questions out loud. That will help you understand where you need to become more polished.

Specialty Sales Representative

This sales rep promotes products in only a few therapeutic areas. Note how seamlessly the physician education component of the job—providing information, setting up seminars, ensuring physicians get their questions answered—fits into the larger sales effort.

Name of position	Pharmaceutical Sales Specialist
Function	Sales
Education level	BS, Biology and Chemistry
Company type and size	Large, public, international pharmaceuticals company
Typical number of hours per week	45 hours

Salary range	$40K—$45K base; bonus: based on meeting goals, percentage (14-16%) of sales goals
Perks	Stock options, extra incentives for meeting goals during product launches or special promotions, special prizes (e.g., trips), company car (includes insurance and mileage allowance)

Responsibilities

I am responsible for selling cardiovascular, respiratory, gastrointestinal and CNS therapeutic products to family practice, internal medicine and specialists relevant to the drug I am representing (cardiologist, neurologist, pulmonologist, allergist, gastroenterologist, etc.). I also have a separate pediatric practice—i.e., I represent my drug to pediatricians. I am expected to do office visits every day of the week—8—10 calls per day. I may have to stop at 15 offices to make that number.

My job has these parts: first, I call on physicians to sell the company's products; second, I provide educational materials for physicians (e.g., low-cholesterol nutrition programs for physicians seeing patients with elevated cholesterol); and third, I put on MD-to-MD education programs that involve gathering a group of doctors at a venue to make presentations on medical topics and disease states relevant to the product. We talk about how the product fits into the disease state. This is especially true with new products. These types of programs are becoming more and more popular—MD-to-MD programs—and proving to be one of the best ways to market our products.

A typical day

8:00 a.m.	Prepare the day. Review my list of physicians to call on and arrange my route.
9:00 a.m.	Office visits Engage in conversations with physicians, make samples available, leave informational materials on products
12:00 p.m.-2:00 p.m.	Offices closed; lunch with staff and/or physicians, great chance to talk to them, catch up on computer work—reports Call in specialist to an office to talk about important issues (e.g., an allergist speaking to physicians about new trends in treatment of allergies, learn about new cases, meet the specialist the MD is referring people to)
2:00 p.m.-5:00 pm	Office visits
5:00 p.m.-6:30 p.m.	Set up an evening event; we usually have one per month. This involves making sure the meeting room is ready (i.e., slide projector, easel for note pad, writing implements, refreshments, etc.)
6:30 p.m.-9:00 p.m.	Host evening event. This involves introducing the speaker(s), moderating the meeting, and making a presentation of how my company's product fits into the disease state that the physician experts are discussing.
9:00 p.m.	Follow up at home (e.g., write up notes, document questions and responses, identify outstanding issues and queries, special needs, etc.)

Uppers and downers

Uppers	Downers
I like the flexibility and the freedom. This is a very good job for a parent, since the flexibility permits me to care for my children and still excel at my job. You don't have to sit in an office. It's constantly changing—no two days are the same. It's good to be independent. There are perks to having a car. The pay is good.	MDs see a lot of reps, but we are sometimes not the most popular persons. Access is sometimes an issue. There's also the big-company bureaucracy to deal with—nothing is ever completed. As soon as you hit a goal, another one is set, so you never feel a sense of completion. You feel like you're chasing a carrot.

Success criteria

You have to be organized. More importantly, you have to be self-driven. On a daily basis, there's no one around to make sure you get up in the morning. So you have to have a good work ethic to earn the rewards, which are definitely there.

Good communication skills are critical. Time management skills are required to handle the workload. You also have to be patient because you are forever hurrying up to get to an office only to have to wait. Most successful reps are assertive. You have to approach interactions purposefully, to not get lost in the buildup.

Advice for jobseekers

New reps need to watch out for physicians asking questions or wandering off the subject such that they won't get to talk about the product itself. It's a kind of good-natured ribbing that is used to test new reps. They'll test your knowledge, push you to see how seriously they can take you. It's part of getting broken into the job.

Some of the most experienced reps say that it takes up to three years to become truly effective in the job. Initially, it's easy to get intimidated by doctors. It takes a while to learn to speak in the physician's language. So, don't get thrown by the jitters at the beginning.

Visit Vault at **www.vault.com** for insider company profiles, expert advice, career message boards, expert resume reviews, the Vault Job Board and more.

VAULT CAREER LIBRARY   **149**

It's a hard industry to get into. One colleague parked in the parking lot of a physician's office and networked with the reps leaving the office. He traded business cards and provided reps with his resume. He was very purposeful and eventually got into a company.

Beware of burnout. Pace yourself. Take time off to recharge. Your job can take over your life since your office is in your house. You have to be able to decide when to call it a day at the end of a day.

Another senior rep had this to say about her job: "It's a very flexible lifestyle—self-directed and self-structured. You can meet family responsibilities. But there's a huge amount of accountability that comes with the job. You have to meet your numbers, make a certain number of calls, deliver a certain message while on the calls, not just show up. Then, there are reports and business analyses of the customers that have to be done. You're essentially running your own business, but with direction."

She also notes that, "the company gives you lists of physicians to see. Within that that territory, it's up to you to figure out how to best use your time. I have a 2-year-old van that already has 50,000 miles on it. I drive 25,000 miles per year. I tend to do a lot of computer work in the evening."

Sales Management

The district sales manager fulfills the first managerial level for a field sales force, is usually drawn from their ranks, and acts as the primary supervisory point of contact for them.

Name of position	District Sales Manager
Function	Sales
Education level	BS, Biology
Company type and size	Large, public, international pharmaceuticals company
Typical number of hours per week	50-55 hours
Salary range	$115K–$140K base; bonus is tied to overall performance of teams under leadership
Perks	Stock options; full benefits package

Responsibilities

As a DM, I have final accountability for meeting the district's sales goals, the district comprising several territories covered by teams of field reps. My other major responsibility is to hire and develop the field force.

To meet this mandate, I develop and implement the business strategy for the district. This involves everything from writing the business plan to being the point person for presenting the company's products to the field force, to ensuring they are properly stocked with information and samples. I keep close tabs on the numbers: sales, expenses, samples, etc. I send detailed reports to middle management periodically.

I meet regularly with the field force to ensure everyone understands the marketing department's positioning for each product, approved product information, and company promotion policies. I also make sure everyone is clear on the industry's marketing code of ethics.

I'm also in the loop with the training department to ensure modules in development are on target and will be effective educational vehicles for the field force. I also interview prospective new hires and write performance reviews for existing reps.

A typical day

7:30 a.m.	Leave home; commute to the office
8:00 a.m.-10:00 a.m.	Check e-mail. Address any requests for information or other inquiries from the field. Check status of quarterly goals
10:00 a.m.-12:00 p.m.	Work on district business plan. Review distribution of samples and information materials to ensure all reps are fully equipped for their sales calls. Review expenses and monitor sales revenues across district.
12:00 p.m.-1:00 pm	Lunch. Attend a lunchtime roundtable discussion of promotion issues given by marketing department. Share specific problems reported to me by field force in addressing physician customers.
1:00 p.m.-3:00 pm	Review resumes and interview prospective new hires. Review interview results with HR and regional manager. Give recommendation for hiring. Prepare performance reviews and development plans for direct reports.

Visit Vault at **www.vault.com** for insider company profiles, expert advice, career message boards, expert resume reviews, the Vault Job Board and more.

VAULT CAREER LIBRARY **151**

3:00 p.m.-5:00 pm	Meet with regional trainer to finalize new hire training program and special topics training for experienced reps. Review and test a new online training module.
5:30 p.m.-6:00 pm	Prepare for and conduct sales team meetings for field reps. Coordinate large events (e.g., symposia, speakers' bureaus, etc.) with designated field reps responsible for organizing the events.
6:00 p.m.	Commute home.
9:00 p.m.-10:00 p.m.	Catch up on reading of trade journals, such as *MedAdvertising News* and *Pharma Executive*

Uppers and downers

Uppers	Downers
I like having a broader impact on meeting company sales goals. It gives me a sense of accomplishment to know that I am promoting products that help people feel better. I also like to develop people, to build their ability to do their jobs, then to see them move forward in their careers. The incentive system works well across the board and that makes my life as a manager easier.	I miss being in the field. I loved calling on customers and listening to their issues. The independence and sense of being my own boss kept me on track. Going to an office every day requires a different set of motivators. You're closer to the pressures other departments are under.

Success criteria

To succeed at being a DM, you have to genuinely like developing people, since that consumes so much of the workweek. In addition, you can't take your eye off the ball. You have to keep people focused on meeting those sales goals. Finally, you have to like the training aspect, since that is a continual and essential part of managing your field force.

Advice for jobseekers

Get in the door as a field rep and spend a few years doing it until you really get the hang of the job. Stick to your original company if possible, since many DMs are hired from the field force. Since being promoted to DM requires both people skills and business skills, you will need strength in both areas. If either one or the other needs to be developed, consider extra training (seminars, courses, etc.) during your personal time to close the gap.

Managed Markets

The managed markets account manager represents the pharmaceutical company to large HMOs and other managed care groups. As such, the job entails business-to-business transactions, as opposed to the business-to-customer contact of field sales reps. The premium here is on developing relationships with key decision makers within the corporate customer organization. Furthermore, account managers work to identify influencers and opinion leaders inside these companies, since the endorsement of these key people will ensure inclusion of the company's products in the formulary.

Name of position	Managed Markets Account Manager
Function	Sales
Education level	BS, Computer Science; MS, Biostatistics
Company type and size	Large, public pharmaceuticals company
Typical number of hours per week	45-50 hours
Salary range	$105K–$140K
Perks	Stock options; full benefits package

Responsibilities

My job has two main aspects: interpersonal and analytical. The interpersonal part involves working within the national account team to support the senior account managers in getting our products accepted into the clients' formularies. Within that context, I also meet with people within the client organization to ensure the account team understands the client's organizational needs, develop volume and pricing schedules, and negotiate other terms of the contracts that are signed with each order.

On the analytical side, most of my responsibilities center around making sure the account team meets specific sales, market share, and return on investment for each client organization. This requires extensive analysis of quantitative data and comprises the "work alone" part of the job. Once these analyses are completed, I formulate and present tactical recommendations to the team leader on how to better meet sales objectives.

A typical day

7:30 a.m.	Commute to office.
8:00 a.m.-9:00 am	Check e-mail. Meet with national account team on a conference call. Discuss my assigned HMO's volume needs for the cardiovasculars market in different regions of the U.S.
9:00 a.m.-12:30 p.m.	Analyze quarterly national sales data. Prepare 6-month report for senior management
12:30 p.m.-1:30 pm	Lunch. Meet with peers in other therapeutic categories (antidepressants and oncology) to share tips on how to apply consultative selling in client organizations.
1:30 p.m.-3:00 pm	Call on internal staff within customer organization, including cardiovasculars medical officer, formulary manager, and group purchasing manager. Discuss new product to be launched within next three months.
3:00 p.m.-5:00 pm	Meet with cross-functional team to map out strategy for new product introduction into the HMO market, including pricing analysts, contract specialists from legal, and product management from marketing. Provide feedback from client contacts.

5:00 p.m.-6:00 p.m.	Manage and monitor quarterly data on reimbursement status, formulary status, restriction of access, and other parameters that impact sales revenues of products already in the managed care market.
6:00 p.m.	Commute home.
9:30 p.m.-10:30 p.m.	Study for day-long Consultative Selling Skills seminar scheduled for the following Saturday.

Uppers and downers

Uppers	Downers
I've always been comfortable with figures, so the data crunching is fun and a good counterpoint to the people-oriented side of the job. The team-based strategy is a great way to approach a corporate client, since relationships are complex and require substantial support. The senior account managers have spent years nurturing clients, and thus provide great role models for someone getting into managed care marketing.	It is sometimes hard to balance the two aspects of the job. Finding several continuous hours to evaluate all the spreadsheets and find the major trends can be challenging, since the team managers can call anytime with client requests. It's also important to stay abreast of the latest analytical technology, and that is a whole other dimension of off-hours work. I have to make sure I make time for that.

Visit Vault at **www.vault.com** for insider company profiles, expert advice, career message boards, expert resume reviews, the Vault Job Board and more.

V/\ULT CAREER LIBRARY   **155**

Success criteria

It is essential to have solid quantitative skills, since the first few years on the job require providing support to the national team. Computing skills are also a must, especially database programs.

If you want to grow in this function, developing the softer skills—negotiating, influencing, closing sales deals—is equally necessary.

The learning is ongoing, and so, a genuine interest in learning will keep you ahead. Finally, teamwork and collaboration are an intrinsic part of the day-to-day work experience.

Advice for jobseekers

Get the foundation in information technology and decide as early as possible what industry you want to work in. That will provide a good deal of clarity. While you are in school, identify projects that involve pharmaceutical and patient data, since that will familiarize you with relevant material.

Any kind of sales experience is a plus. Don't be reluctant to start with a job in an IT support function, since that will broaden your foundation in understanding database applications.

Marketing Management

The product manager gets a product to market. As "owner" and "champion" of the product, the product manager builds the brand associated with the product and presents his or her vision of the brand to others functions within the company. Product managers also take the lead in approving the advertising campaign to promote the product.

Name of position	Associate Product Manager
Function	Marketing
Education level	BS, Molecular Biology; MBA, Marketing
Company type and size	Large, global pharmaceuticals company
Typical number of hours per week	50-55 hours
Salary range	$120K–$150K
Perks	Stock options; full benefits package

Responsibilities

I develop the strategy for launching a product, in my case in the oncology area. This means I am responsible for thinking about all aspects of introducing a new cancer drug in the marketplace. I also take the lead in implementing the strategy.

A lot of planning goes with this job. As part of the marketing plan, I analyze the market for the oncology area of the company, do a competitor analysis, profile customers, recommend how to best position the product and monitor how it is doing against its leading competitors.

I also provide consulting advice on the product for anyone in the company who might need to understand the business aspects of a drug. For example, I'll provide growth trend estimates on a new oncology drug to treat lymphatic cancer or present the latest results on whether that product can be used to treat related cancers, and it turn, how that will impact overall sales revenues for the product.

The last—but certainly not least—part of my job is to maintain the product team's spirit, often through years of shepherding the drug through clinical trials and regulatory submissions. We have a lot of hurdles to clear and I make sure we stay on track.

A typical day

7:30 a.m.	Leave home; commute to the office
8:00 a.m.-10:00 a.m.	Check e-mail. Review comments and other information from various departments—marketing research, regulatory affairs, sales management, etc.—on the oncology products quarterly marketing plan. Then, I incorporate their information into the main draft and submit the plan to my manager (the senior marketing manager, who manages all oncology product marketing).
10:00 a.m.-12:00 p.m.	Meet with advertising group to review promotion materials for upcoming launch. Suggest revisions based on revised positioning statement. Confirm final language of approved indications with regulatory affairs manager.
12:00 p.m.-12:45 pm	Participate in international conference call on strategy for simultaneous launch in North America, the UK, and European Union. Discuss timing and strategy for entry into emerging markets (China, India, and South America).

Visit Vault at www.vault.com for insider company profiles, expert advice, career message boards, expert resume reviews, the Vault Job Board and more.

VAULT CAREER LIBRARY 157

12:45 p.m.-2:00 pm	Attend a brown bag lunch with new and recent hires to listen to their concerns and provide individual advice and encouragement.
2:00 p.m.-4:00 pm	Meet with cross-functional product team (sales, regulatory affairs, manufacturing, training, legal, and finance) to review product launch plans for U.S., UK, and EU. Finalize time line for product introduction.
4:00 p.m.-5:30 pm	Review training program developed by training manager for new oncology drug. Test new online modules. Review product knowledge module.
5:30 p.m.-6:00 pm	Collect and read latest marketing research competitive intelligence report.
6:00 p.m.-6:30 p.m.	Meet with senior marketing manager to review preliminary plans for introduction of two product line extensions within the next 6 to 12 months in order to extend patent protection period.
6:30 p.m.	Commute home.
10:00 p.m.-11:00 pm	Read *Wall Street Journal* Health section on pharmaceutical industry.

Uppers and downers

Uppers	Downers
The scope of responsibilities of my job crates a strong entrepreneurial experience. It's like being the chief executive of your own little company. I love building a brand image. It's creative but within a context of getting a specific message across. I also like being the go-to person for my product within the company. It keeps me motivated to develop and maintain a high level of expertise, so that I can answer everyone's questions.	There's a lot of stress, having to juggle a lot of balls in the air all at once, making sure everything is on track for launch. In recent years, we've had to launch simultaneously in big markets, so the logistics can be quite challenging. Also. I'm responsible for getting bottom line results, which makes it essential that my analysis be correct. I spend a lot of time ensuring that our business expectations are aligned with the realities of the market. That can translate into extra hours.

Success criteria

To be a successful product manager, you have to be able to see the big picture, to understand all the pieces of activity that have to fall into place to introduce a product into the marketplace successfully. At the same time, it is essential to have a command of the details, the numbers, and to be able to communicate with people in all departments within the company.

We try to minimize uncertainty, but that is seldom on an absolute level. Hence, you have to become comfortable making reasonable guesstimates. Then, when circumstances require it, a dose of flexibility is most helpful.

One other important key is to delegate—ensure that people have clear direction on what their responsibilities are and when work is due. Finally, I've found that it helps to be a diplomat—to persuade, influence, and promote your plan.

Advice for jobseekers

Build both hard analytical and soft interpersonal skills simultaneously. Get advanced business education—that is a virtual must-have these days. Although no one expects you to understand the science as well as a researcher or clinician, it is to your advantage to understand as much science as possible.

To break into a marketing job, internships are certainly the best way to go, but many people start out as field reps. By getting primary exposure to physician and pharmacy customers, the marketing analytics data makes much more sense. Field experience ultimately gives you more insight into customer needs.

Marketing Support: Sales Training

The sales trainer is often drawn from the best field reps, those who have shown an exceptional grasp of product knowledge, company policies, and customer relations. Generally, trainers have very strong interpersonal relations and are natural extroverts. Many spend as much as 50% of their time in direct contact with learners.

Visit Vault at **www.vault.com** for insider company profiles, expert advice, career message boards, expert resume reviews, the Vault Job Board and more.

VAULT CAREER LIBRARY   159

Name of position	Regional Sales Trainer Pharmaceutical Executive Sales Representative
Function	Sales
Education level	BS, Biology; MBA, Sales and Marketing
Company type and size	Large, public, international pharmaceuticals company
Typical number of hours per week	45-55 hours
Salary range	$90K—$120K base
Perks	Stock options; full benefits package

Responsibilities

My job centers on supporting the field sales organization by creating and implementing the training programs needed to ensure the field force understands the company's promotion strategy for its key products, its marketing policies, and the utilization of the products themselves in different patient populations.

I accomplish this mission via a host of vehicles. Our programs increasingly use Web-based learning to achieve our objectives, but in addition to e-learning, we continue to have classroom training programs, home-study print materials, audio and video tapes, and workshops, which include interactive games and other fun activities to solidify the reps' understanding of the scientific and medical information.

A typical day

7:45 a.m.	Leave home; commute to the office
8:00 a.m.-9:00 a.m.	Check e-mail. Respond to queries for assistance from field reps on home-study print program. Review notes for training delivery. Check classroom for readiness.
9:00 a.m.-12:00 p.m.	Deliver training program for new hires.
12:00 p.m.-1:00 p.m.	Attend a lunchtime seminar with other regional trainers to discuss tips on classroom training effectiveness. Note ideas to implement.

1:00 p.m.-3:00 p.m.	Work on regional training needs assessment. Identify areas that have greatest needs. Revise training practices and policies. Monitor and provide new hire training performance data to training management.
3:00 p.m.-5:00 p.m.	Meet with district manager to review new hire training program and special topics training for experienced reps. Introduce DM and marketing department product team members to a new online training module.
5:30 p.m.-6:00 p.m.	Prepare for and conduct Train-the-Trainer meetings for new trainers. Prepare for regional training meeting for next quarter. Coordinate meeting site arrangements.
6:00 p.m.	Commute home.
9:00 p.m.-10:00 p.m.	Read trade journals, such as *Training* magazine and online learning newsletters.

Uppers and downers

Uppers	Downers
I love teaching—the people connection that comes with the classroom experience. Many new hires are frankly stressed about passing the tests we give them to qualify for entering the field. I like easing them through the program into the field, where they can make the impact they want so much. Also, teaching is a great vehicle for learning. I stay on my toes with all the issues impacting the sales force—everything from product knowledge to the new marketing code to helping integrate technology in the sales process.	I came from the field and sometimes I miss being out there. Although we had to make a quota of calls everyday, I still felt I could operate independently. The classroom part of a training job is very structured, and multi-day programs require a lot of stamina. I'm more careful about keeping in shape so I can make it through the long days.

Visit Vault at **www.vault.com** for insider company profiles, expert advice, career message boards, expert resume reviews, the Vault Job Board and more.

VAULT CAREER LIBRARY **161**

Success criteria

Excellent people skills are essential to succeed in this job, since there is virtually no downtime from people-oriented responsibilities. Because of that, it is also very important to be well organized, to find and dispatch information quickly and to manage time well.

Because an increasing share of the actual training is being delivered through technology, it helps to have an affinity for the computer—for its potential in creating efficiencies in getting the work done from my end as well as in delivering an effective learning experience for the field reps.

Advice for jobseekers

Get the foundation first, then move into teaching. This means learn what the life sciences are about, to the point of becoming completely comfortable with the vocabulary of human physiology and pathology. Next, get a business orientation: we bring products to market. This means becoming equally comfortable with the language of business. Put the two together; find people who find this an easy and pleasurable exercise. Then prove yourself. The sheer ease and mastery with which you make your presentations will set you apart. Even if you don't want to train forever, doing a rotation in the training department can be most valuable.

Corporate Culture

CHAPTER 13

Most Big Pharma companies lean conservative. Big Biotech companies—which we have noted are essentially mid-cap pharmaceutical companies—have more in common with Big Pharma than many of them would admit. Cultural differences among pharmaceutical companies can be classified along three dimensions:

• Type of organization: functionally integrated vs. specialty business units

• Origin of top leadership: Foreign vs. American-owned

• Scope of integration: research shops vs. full infrastructure

Type of Organization

The functionally integrated organization

Most Big Pharma companies are functionally integrated. They have traditional hierarchies, with executive vice presidents in each main area—R&D, sales, marketing, manufacturing, administration, and human resources. These same companies have been mostly responsible for the "blockbuster" drugs, products generating at least $1 billion in sales. The largest pharmaceutical company in the world, Pfizer, is currently organized by functional area.

The marketing in these companies is aggressive and increasingly directed at the consumer. An important component of marketing strategy is to expand the reach of a successful drug—obtain approval for new indications, create combination formulas with other drugs to extend the patent protection period, or create new dosage and delivery mechanisms. The underlying purpose is to sell the product to as many patients as possible. Sales forces are aggressive, competitive, and highly polished. The culture of these marketing-driven organizations reflects their primary business model. Marketing people get involved early in product development teams and influence what products do come to market.

The crisis brought on by the near-demise of the Cox-2 inhibitors highlights the larger problem with mass-marketed drugs. In April 2005, Pfizer announced a major restructuring, which should yield savings in operations of several billion dollars over the next few years. Later in 2005, Pfizer announced it would not reduce its massive sales force, suggesting that the existing force will have to be re-deployed to create more value per rep. At mid-decade, traditional Big Pharma sales forces are being slowly transitioned into forces that promote drugs that are targeted at smaller patient populations and with a narrower profile of approved indications—in other words, into specialty reps.

The specialty business unit organization

Many biotech companies and some Big Pharma ones (e.g., Johnson & Johnson, Novartis, Genzyme) have organized their pharmaceutical units around therapeutic specialty areas, each with their own sales forces and profit centers. Essentially the "Oncology Group" or the "Respiratory Therapy Group" are mini-businesses, and sales reps focus only on products in their group. In such cases, target patient groups are substantially smaller than for the mass-marketed drugs. Here, the group has the feel of a small business, and there is a greater chance to learn about all aspects of launching a drug faster than in a traditional company.

In rare diseases with small patient groups, the sales rep takes on a more nuanced role, serving more of a medical information consultant than as a sales agent. Over time, the rep becomes part of the extended team of caregivers and even gets to know patients themselves. Such a culture is more collaborative, less overtly aggressive, and places a greater premium on building and maintaining relationships. Make no mistake, the company will still set sales goals and expect its field force to meet them, but there is a more personal feel to the job.

Origin of Top Leadership

U.S. affiliates of foreign companies

Most Big Pharma companies are global and in some cases, the ownership is foreign and corporate headquarters outside the U.S. Examples include Novartis (Swiss), Schering AG (German), AstraZeneca (Swedish), and GlaxoSmithKline (United Kingdom). Although most U.S. subsidiaries retain an American character, you will likely find that senior management leans distinctly toward the country of ownership. How that impacts the corporate cultures is subtle, but palpable. Most foreign-owned companies tend to be more conservative socially—i.e., they lack the first-name familiarity that is common in American-owned corporations. Indeed, many Europeans find this aspect of American business culture annoying by varying degrees.

To solve this problem, one safe tactic is to be alert to how people around you refer to their superiors, especially to the company's executive team. Take your cues from them. Another safe bet is to begin with a more formal stance, then move to a more informal posture, once you have been given permission. Note that that this approach is much less awkward than doing the reverse. If you are still unsure, don't be afraid to ask.

Scope of Integration

Discovery research-based organizations

Still another variant of corporate cultures are companies which are primarily focused on research and early-stage product development. Most of these companies are small biotechs. They do not have fully established sales and marketing infrastructure. In such cases, the science is the core of the company's assets and its scientific staff is driving the leadership of the company.

The "marketing function" is subsumed under "business development," and is essentially a medium for acquiring licensing deals with big drug distributors. If you choose to work for one of these companies, you will have a much smaller pool of peers with whom to interact. You can expect the scientific perspective to be prevalent, with the chief scientists having the greatest prestige. Still, the atmosphere in these companies is the most casual. As one scientist notes, "my company is more laid-back than some others."

Visit Vault at **www.vault.com** for insider company profiles, expert advice,
career message boards, expert resume reviews, the Vault Job Board and more.

V/\ULT CAREER LIBRARY   **165**

VAULT

THE MOST TRUSTED NAME IN CAREER INFORMATION

Vault guides and employer profiles have been published since 1997 and are the premier source of insider information on careers.

Each year, Vault surveys and interviews thousands of employees to give readers the inside scoop on industries and specific employers to help them get the jobs they want.

VAULT

Final Analysis

At the end of 2005, two newspaper stories appeared within days of each other, both illustrating stark realities in the world of pharmaceutical marketing. The first paraphrased headline was, "Merck to cut 7,000 jobs; will not say if Sales force to take hit." The second: "Cheerleaders enliven pharmaceutical sales." What's happening here?

At this writing, neither Merck nor industry-leader Pfizer are tipping their hand on the size of the sales force—the traditional entry point for many pharmaceutical marketing careers. Some industry observers speculate that culling is inevitable; others claim that existing forces will be slowly transitioned to specialty sales.

Meanwhile, physicians' lives in the other story are spiced up with attractive, outgoing female reps recruited from the ranks of cheerleaders at large universities, more on their looks and personality than academic achievement. The premise is that good looks and an extroverted, amiable temperament—be they on females or males—are the keys to a drug rep's success.

If you've made it to these concluding thoughts, you're likely to have a genuine interest in the industry. So here's the bottom line:

Appearance: Everyone—and I do mean everyone—who comes into contact with clients must be exquisitely groomed—every day!! Male and female, young, old, and in-between. There are no exceptions and no Casual Fridays.

Temperament: Given those 8 to 10 calls you have to make every day, five days a week, you will be happier and more productive if you are a natural extrovert. Furthermore, you need to have a high threshold for rejection (to deal with over-burdened doctors) and be well-organized (to track all those samples).

Knowledge: Neither appearance nor temperament alone will enable you to succeed in the emerging industry. Specialized knowledge is at a premium and specialty products likely to take up a greater proportion of the industry's portfolio in coming years. So study hard, learn a life science, and develop your interpersonal skills. If you are early in your career, identify areas of improvement, and invest in your professional development.

The industry's biotech labs have dozens of innovative new products in clinical trials, ones that promise to improve the lives of millions of people. It will be your privilege to bring these products to those who need them. The future of biopharmaceutical marketing is indeed exciting.

APPENDIX

Appendix

Resources in Pharmaceutical Sales and Marketing

Employment sites

Innovex: contract sales company
www.innovexglobal.net

Nelson: contract sales company
www.nelsonprofessionalsales.com

Professional Detailing, Inc. (PDI): contract sales company
www.pdi-inc.com

PRP Consulting, Inc.: recruiter focusing on pharmaceutical sales
www.prp-consulting.com

Direct Employers: direct recruiting site organized by a group of large corporations; find pharmaceutical companies using keywords "drug" or "pharmaceuticals"
www.directemployers.com

Medical information

FDA approval process outline: overview of agency's steps in approving a drug for sale in the U.S.
www.msajobs.com/DrugDisc.htm

Cancer Web: cluster of links on everything relating to cancer.
www.cancerweb.com

CenterWatch Clinical Trials Listing Service: Clinical trials details; a good place to learn about the status of potential new products and where they stand in the FDA approval process.
www.centerwatch.com

CDER New Drug Approvals: recent FDA drug approvals.
www.fda.gov/cder/approval/index.htm

IMS Health: authoritative healthcare information provider
www.imshealth.com

Visit Vault at **www.vault.com** for insider company profiles, expert advice,
career message boards, expert resume reviews, the Vault Job Board and more.

VAULT CAREER LIBRARY   **171**

Hoovers Online: company research; good place to bone up on specific companies before interviews.
www.hoovers.com

Online and print publications

Drugtopics.com: Online publication associated with the longest-running pharmacy publication in America
www.Drugtopics.com

PharmRep: Online magazine largely written by pharmaceutical reps; a great source of insights into issues facing field sales forces
www.pharmrep.com/

MediConf: Lists over 10,000 future events including conferences, workshops, seminars, symposia and exhibitions in medicine, healthcare, pharmacology and biotechnology
www.mediconf.de/

Standard & Poor's Industry Surveys, published bi-annually by Standard & Poor's, a leading provider of financial and business information; available in reference business and social science libraries

Books

Pharmaceutical Resource Center, Pharmaceutical Sales Interview Survival Guide, Austin, TX 2004, (www.PharmaceuticalSalesHelp.com)

Jane Williams, Insider's Guide to the World of Pharmaceutical Sales, 7th Edition, Principle Publications, Arlington, TX 2004, (www.principle publications.com)

Physician's Desk Reference (PDR). Offers scientific information on major disease groups and the drugs available to treat them. A good introduction to the science behind a class of drugs marketed by a company you are interviewing.

Medical Journals

Journal of the American Medical Association: prestigious scientific publication from the major physician trade group

Journal of the American Medical Association

Journal of the National Cancer Institute: scientific journal with the latest on cancer research and cancer-fighting drugs

Journal of the National Cancer Institute

Journal of Infectious Diseases: scientific journal with the latest on dreaded viral and other infectious diseases
www.journals.uchicago.edu

Trade groups

America's Health Insurance Plans: trade group that represents managed care companies
www.ahip.org

American Society of Health-System Pharmacists
www.ashp.org

Biotechnology Industry Organization: major industry site for biotech industry
www.bio.org

Certified Medical Representative Institute: resource for continuing education and credential development for industry reps
www.cmr.org

PhRMA: Leading industry trade group; site contains summaries of main issues, recent news and information
www.phrma.org

Society of Pharmaceutical and Biotech Trainers: good reference site for training trends within the industry
www.spbt.org

Government

Agency for Health Care Policy and Research: a good site for the latest thinking on healthcare policy discourse
www.ahcpr.gov

Centers for Disease Control and Prevention: the prestigious, Atlanta-based agency charged with studying infectious diseases and how to best protect the public from them
www.cdc.gov

Visit Vault at **www.vault.com** for insider company profiles, expert advice, career message boards, expert resume reviews, the Vault Job Board and more.

VAULT CAREER LIBRARY   **173**

Food and Drug Administration: the main regulatory agency for the pharmaceutical industry
www.fda.gov

Health Care Finance Association: gives the latest thinking on how to reform our system
www.hcfa.gov

National Center for Health Statistics: the CDC's statistical arm, this site provides access to disease statistics; useful in estimating a drug's potential market size.
www.cdc.gov/nchs/nvss.htm

Top Pharmaceutical Employers

3M Canada
3M Center/Building #225-1S-15
St. Paul, MN 55144-1000
US
Phone: (800) 328-0255
www.mmm.com

Abbott Laboratories
100 Abbottt Park Rd.
Abbott Park, IL 60064-3500
US
Phone: (800) 255-5162
www.abbott.com

Alcon Laboratories
6201 S Freeway
Fort Worth, TX 76134
US
Phone: (817) 293-0450
www.alconlabs.com

Allergan
255 DuPont Drive
Irvine, CA 92612
US
Phone: (800) 347-4500
www.allergan.com

Ascent Pediatrics
187 Ballardvale Street
Wilmington, MA 01887
US
Phone: (978) 658-2500
www.ascentpediatrics.com

AstraZeneca
1800 Concord Pike
Wilmington, DE 19850-F315
US
Phone: (610) 695-1000
www.astrazeneca-us.com

Aventis Pharmaceuticals
300 Somerset Corporate Boulevard
Bridgewater, NJ 08807-2854
US
Phone: (800) 891-2491
www.aventis.com

Axcan Pharma, Inc.
597 Laurier Blvd
Mont Saint Hilaire, QC J3H 6C4
CA
Phone: (450) 467-5138
www.axcan.com

Berlex Laboratories
300 Fairfield Rd.
Wayne, NJ 07470
US
Phone: (973) 694-4100
www.berlex.com

Bertek Pharmaceuticals, Inc.
530 Davis Drive
Durham, NC 27713
US
Phone: (888) 523-7835
www.bertek.com

Bioglan Pharma
7 Great Valley Pkwy
Malvern, PA 19355
US
Phone: (610) 232-2000
www.bioglan.com

Biovail Pharmaceuticals, Inc.
170 Southport Drive
Morrisville, NC 27560
Phone: (866) 246-8245
www.biovailpharm.com

Visit Vault at **www.vault.com** for insider company profiles, expert advice,
career message boards, expert resume reviews, the Vault Job Board and more.

VAULT CAREER LIBRARY   **175**

Boehringer Ingelheim Canada
5180 South Service Road
Burlington, ON L7L 5H4
CA
Phone: (905) 639-0333
www.boehringer-ingelheim.ca

Boehringer Ingelheim Corp.
900 Ridgebury Rd.
Ridgefield, CT 06877
US
Phone: (800) 542-6257
www.boehringer-ingelheim.com

Braintree Laboratories
P.O. Box 850929
Braintree, MA 02185-0929
US
Phone: (781) 843-2202
www.braintreelabs.com

BYK Canada
1275 N Service Road West
Oakville, ON L6M 3G4
CA
Phone: (908) 469-9333
www.bykcanada.com

Celltech Pharmaceuticals
755 Jefferson Road
Rochester, NY 14623
US
Phone: (716) 475-9000
www.chrioscience.com

Connaught Laboratories
Route 611
Swiftwater, PA 18370
US
Phone: (800) 822-2463
www.connaught.com

Connetics Corporation
3294 West Bayshore Rd
Palo Alto, CA 94303-4013
US
Phone: (650) 843-2800
www.connetics.com

Daiichi Pharmaceutical Corporation
11 Phillips Parkway
Montvale, NJ 07645
US
Phone: (877)324-4244
www.daiichius.com

Dermik Laboratories
500 Arcola Ln.
Collegeville, PA 19426-0107
US
Phone: (610) 454-8000
www.dermik.com

Dey Laboratories
2751 Napa Valley Corporate Dr.
Napa, CA 94558
US
Phone: (800) 869-9005
www.deyinc.com

Eisai Co., Ltd.
500 Frank W. Burr Blvd.
Teaneck, NJ 07666-6741
US
Phone: (888) 274-2378
www.eisai.com

Elan Pharmaceuticals
800 Gateway Blvd.
South San Francisco, CA 94080
US
Phone: (650) 877-0900
www.elancorp.com

Eli Lilly and Company
Lilly Corporate Center
Indianapolis, IN 46285
US
Phone: (317) 276-2000
www.lilly.com

Endo Pharmaceuticals
223 Wilmington West Chester
Pike
Chadds Ford, PA 19317
US
Phone: (610) 558-9800
www.endo.com

Essentia Pharmaceuticals
16690 Swingle Ridge
Chesterfield, MO 63017
US
Phone: (636) 536-4500
www.essentia-pharm.com

Ferndale Laboratories, Inc.
780 W Eight Mile Road
Ferndale, MI 48220
US
Phone: (248) 548-0900
www.ferndalelabs.com

Ferring Pharmaceuticals, Inc.
400 Rella Blvd
Suffern, NY 10901
US
Phone: (845) 770-2600
www.ferring.com

First Horizon Pharmaceuticals
660 Hembree Pkwy
Fort Worth, TX 76111
US
Phone: (800) 441-8227
www.horizonpharm.com

Forest Pharmaceuticals, Inc.
13622 Lakefront Dr.
St. Louis, MO 63045
US
Phone: (314) 344-8870
www.forestlabs.com

Fujisawa USA, Inc.
Parkway North Center
Deerfield, IL 60015
US
Phone: (847) 317-8800
www.fujisawa.com

Gate Pharmaceuticals
1090 Horshman Rd
North Wales, PA 19454
US
Phone: (800) 292-4293
www.gatepharma.com

GlaxoSmithKline
Five Moore Dr.
Research Triangle Park, NC
27709
US
Phone: (888) 825-5249
www.gsk.com

Healthpoint Phamaceuticals
2600 Airport Freeway
Fort Worth, TX 76111
US
Phone: (800) 441-8227
www.healthpoint.com

ICN Pharmaceuticals
3300 Hyland Avenue
Costa Mesa, CA 92626
US
Phone: (714) 545-0100
www.icnpharm.com

Visit Vault at **www.vault.com** for insider company profiles, expert advice,
career message boards, expert resume reviews, the Vault Job Board and more.

VAULT CAREER LIBRARY　　**177**

Immunex
51 University St.
Seattle, WA 98101
US
Phone: (800) 466-8639
www.immunex.com

Innovex
Waterview Corporate Centre
Parsippany, NJ 07054
US
Phone: (973) 257-4500
www.innovexglobal.com

**Integrity Pharmaceutical
Corporation**
9084 Technology Drive
Fishers, IN 46038
US
Phone: (800) 823-6878
www.colofresh.com

Ivax Corporation
4400 Biscayne Blvd
Miami, FL 33137
US
Phone: (800) 980-4829
www.ivax.com

Janssen Pharmaceutica
1125 Trenton-Harbourton Rd.
Titusville, NJ 08560-0200
US
Phone: (800) 526-7736
www.us.janssen.com

Key Pharmaceuticals, Inc.
Galloping Hill Rd.
Kenilworth, NJ 07033
US
Phone: (908) 298-4000
www.keypharmaceuticals.com

Knoll Pharmaceutical Co.
3000 Continental Drive North
Mount Olive, NJ 07828-1234
US
Phone: (800) 526-0710

Leo Pharma
123 Commerce Valley East
Thornhill, ON L3T 7W8
CA
Phone: (905) 427-8828
www.leo-pharma.com

McKesson HBOC
One Post Street
San Francisco, CA 94104-5296
US
Phone: (415) 983-8300

McNeil Consumer Healthcare
7050 Camp Hill Road
Fort Washington, PA 19034
US
Phone: (215) 273-7000
www.mcneilcampusrecruiting.com

Medicis
8125 North Hayden Raod
Scottsdale, AZ 85258
US
Phone: (480) 808-8800
www.medicis.com

Merck & Co., Inc.
1 Merck Drive
Whitehouse Station, NJ 08889
US
Phone: (908) 423-1000
www.merck.com

MGI Pharma
Suite 300 E.
Minnetonka, MN 55343-9667
US
Phone: (612) 346-4700
www.mgipharma.com

Miles Pharmaceutical
400 Morgan Lane
West Haven, CT 06516
US
Phone: (203) 937-2000

Monarch Pharmaceuticals
501 Fifth Street
Bristol, TN 37620
US
Phone: (423) 989-8000
www.monarchpharm.com

Muro Pharmaceuticals, Inc.
890 East St.
Tewksbury, MA 01876-1496
US
Phone: (800) 225-0974
www.muropharm.com

Novartis Pharmaceuticals Corp.
59 Route 10
East Hanover, NJ 07936-1080
US
Phone: (888) 669-6682
www.novartis.com

Noven Pharmaceuticals
11960 SW 144th Street
Miami, FL 33186
US
Phone: (305) 253-5099
www.noven.com

Novo Nordisk Pharmaceuticals, Inc.
100 College Road West
Princeton, NJ 08540
US
Phone: (609) 987-5800
www.novonordisk.com

Organon, Inc.
375 Mt. Pleasant Ave
West Orange, NJ 07052
US
Phone: (800) 241-8812
www.organon.com

Ortho Biotech, Inc.
700 Route 202 South
Raritan, NJ 08869
US
Phone: (908) 704-5000
www.orthobiotech.com

Ortho McNeil Pharmaceutical
1000 Route 202 South
Raritan, NJ 08869-0602
US
Phone: (800) 682-6532
www.ortho-mcneil.com

Otsuka America Pharmaceutical, Inc.
2440 Research Blvd.
Rockville, MD 20850
US
Phone: (301) 990-0030
www.otsuka.com

Pathogenesis Corporation
5215 Old Orchard Rd
Skokie, IL 60071
US
Phone: (847) 583-8050
www.chiron.com

Visit Vault at www.vault.com for insider company profiles, expert advice,
career message boards, expert resume reviews, the Vault Job Board and more.

VAULT CAREER LIBRARY   179

PediaMed Pharmaceuticals
782 Springdale Drive
Exton, PA 19341
US
Phone: (484) 875-9375
www.pediamedpharma.com

Pfizer, Inc.
235 East 42nd St.
New York, NY 10017
US
Phone: (212) 573-2323
www.pfizer.com

**Procter & Gamble
Pharmaceuticals**
One Proctor & Gamble Plaza
Cincinnati, OH 45202
US
Phone: (800) 448-4878
www.pg.com

Professional Detailing, Inc.
10 Mountainview Road
Upper Saddle River, NJ 07458
US
Phone: (201) 818-8450
www.pdi-inc.om

Purdue Pharma
One Stamford Forum
Stamford, CT 06901-3431
US
Phone: (203) 588-8000
www.purduepharma.com

Reliant Pharmaceuticals
Route 202/206 South
Bridgewater, NJ 08807
US
Phone: (908) 580-1200
www.reliantrx.com

Ross Products Division
625 Cleveland Ave
Columbus, OH 43215-1724
US
Phone: (800) 986-8510
www.ross.com

Salix Pharmaceuticals, Ltd.
8540 Colonnade Center Drive
Releigh, NC 27615
US
Phone: (919) 862-1000
www.salixltd.com

Sankyo Pharma
Two Hilton Court
Parsippany, NJ 07054
US
Phone: (973) 359-2600
www.sankyopharma.com

Sanofi-Synthelabo
90 Park Av.
New York, NY 10016
US
Phone: (212) 551.4000
www.sanofi-synthelabo.com

Santen, Inc.
555 Gateway Drive
Napa, CA 94558
US
Phone: (707) 254-1750
www.santen.com

Savage Laboratories
60 Baylis Rd.
Melville, NY 11747
US
Phone: (800) 231-0206
www.savagelabs.com

Scandipharm, Inc.
22 Inverness Center Pkwy
Birmingham, AL 35242
US
Phone: (800) 950-8085
www.axcanscandipharm.com

Schering-Plough Corp.
One Giralda Farms
Madison, NJ 07940-1010
US
Phone: (973) 822-7000
www.schering-plough.com

Schwarz Pharma, Inc.
P.O. Box 2038
Milwaukee, WI 53201
US
Phone: (414) 354-4300
www.schwarzusa.com

Sepracor, Inc.
111 Locke Drive
Marlborough, MA 01752
US
Phone: (508) 357-7300
www.sepracor.com

Serono Laboratories, Inc.
100 Longwater Circle
Nowell, MA 02061
US
Phone: (888) 398-4567
www.seronousa.com

Servier Canada, Inc.
235 Blvd Armand-Frappier
Laval, QC H7V 4A7
CA
Phone: (450) 978-9700
www.servier.com

Shire Richwood Pharmaceuticals
7900 Tanners Gate Dr
Florence, KY 41042
US
Phone: (859) 282-2100
www.shiregroup.com

Sigma Tau Pharmaceuticals
800 South Frederick Av.
Gaithersburg, MD 20877
US
Phone: (301) 948-1041
www.sigmatau.com

SmithKline Beecham
One Franklin Plaza
Philadelphia, PA 19101
US
Phone: (800)366-8900
www.sb.com

Solvay Pharmaceuticals, Inc.
901 Sawyer Rd.
Marietta, GA 30062
US
Phone: (770) 578-9000
www.solvay.com

Stiefel Laboratories, Inc.
255 Alhambra Circle
Coral Gables, FL 33134
US
Phone: (888) 784-3335
www.stiefel.com

**Takeda Pharmaceuticals
America, Inc.**
475 Half Day Road
Lincolnshire, IL 60089
US
Phone: (847) 382-3000
www.takedapharm.com

Visit Vault at **www.vault.com** for insider company profiles, expert advice,
career message boards, expert resume reviews, the Vault Job Board and more.

VAULT CAREER LIBRARY   **181**

TAP Pharmaceutical Products, Inc.
675 North Field Drive
Lake Forest, IL 60045
US
Phone: (800) 621-1020
www.tap.co

UCB Pharma, Inc.
1950 Lake Park Dr.
Smyrna, GA 30080
US
Phone: (800) 477-7877
www.ucb.com

Upsher-Smith Laboratories, Inc.
13700 1st Avenue North
Minneapolis, MN 55441
US
Phone: (800) 654-2299
www.upsher-smith.com

Wallace Labratories
www.wallacelabs.com

Warner Chilcott
Rockaway 80 Corporate Center
Rockaway, NJ 07886
US
Phone: (973) 442-3200
www.wclabs.com

Watson Pharmaceuticals
311 Bonnie Circle
Corona, CA 91720
US
Phone: (800) 272-5525
www.watsonpharm.com

Womens First Healthcare
12220 El Camino Real
San Diego, CA 92130
US
Phone: (858) 509-1171
www.womensfirst.com

Wyeth-Ayerst Laboratories
555 Lancaster Avenue
St Davids, PA 19087
US
Phone: (610) 902-1200
www.wyeth.com

Internship Information

Company sources of internships

Abbott Laboratories

100 Abbott Park Road
Abbott Park, Illinois 60064-6400
Tel: 847-937-6100
Internet: www.abbott.com

One of the leading companies in the industry, with over 50,000 employees working in 130 countries and annual sales greater than $10 billion, Abbott Laboratories produces and markets pharmaceuticals, diagnostics and hospital supplies. Abbott offers over 100 internships in a variety of areas including Research and Development, Engineering, Finance, Operations, Sales, Technology and Human Resources.

Internships last 12 weeks over the summer semester and provide first-hand experience in both ongoing and project-oriented work. The company looks for candidates with majors in Engineering, Computer Science, Business, Finance, Marketing, Accounting, Human Resources, and Life Sciences. MBAs are also attractive candidates.

Application deadline is in February for an internship later in the summer. Applicants should include their grade point average and whether they've had previous internships. All internships come with a competitive stipend. Online applications are accepted at www.abbott.com/career/.

Over 250 college students participated in Abbott's internship program in 2004. Over 40% of those eligible for hiring were in fact hired as full-time employees. Abbott provides housing for interns who live over 40 miles from their internship site at facilities that offer a variety of services and access to athletic facilities.

Abbott's Summer Internship Program has been rated as one of America's Top 100 Internships by the The Princeton Review, a New York based education services company, since 1994, as well as one of the best companies for recent graduates. Be sure to check out Princeton's recently published book, Best Entry Level Jobs for more information.

Visit Vault at **www.vault.com** for insider company profiles, expert advice,
career message boards, expert resume reviews, the Vault Job Board and more.

VAULT CAREER LIBRARY **183**

Boeringer Ingelheim
Boehringer Ingelheim Pharmaceuticals, Inc.
900 Ridgebury Road/P.O. Box 368
Ridgefield, CT 06877
Tel: 203.798.9988
Internet: http://us.boehringer-ingelheim.com/employment/interns.htm

Boehringer Ingelheim accepts internship applications from undergraduate, graduate, and MBA students. For local internships, contact the Human Resources department in the country where you reside. See www.boehringer-ingelheim.com/corporate/career/internships.htm.

Internships are available for college students who are sophomores or beyond, have completed at least four courses in their major field, have earned at least a 3.3 grade point average, and are eligible to work in the U.S. Applicants with majors in Chemistry, Biology, Chemical Engineering, Pharmaceutics, Pharmaceutical Sciences, Animal Sciences, Computer Science, and Medical and Health Economics are attractive candidates.

Boeringer-Ingelheim also offers international internships, preferably for applicants with successful previous internships and who possess relevant language skills. For these internships, contact corporateHR@boeringer-ingelheim.com or at www.boehringer-ingelheim.com/ corporate/career/job_ opportunities.htm.

Boston Scientific Corporation
Ms. Jennifer Farabine
University Relations
Boston Scientific Corporation
1 Boston Scientific Place
Natick, Massachusetts 01760
Internet: www.bostonscientific.com

Boston Scientific Corporation (BSC) is the world leader in the design and manufacture of less intrusive medical devices. They offer 125 internships annually in areas including Engineering, Strategic Planning, Research and Development and Financial Structures. The company prefers applicants with majors in Engineering, Finance, and the Life Sciences. MBA students are also attractive applicants.

Most internships last from 10 to 12 weeks over the summer semester, although a few are granted during the academic year. The experience includes a variety of on-the-job training, seminars, professional development classes, and social events.

© 2006 Vault Inc.

Internships come with stipends of variable amounts. Since they are available for all three semesters, the company has rolling application deadlines per semester. You may apply online at http:www.bostonscientific.com.

Johnson & Johnson Family of Companies
Internship Coordinator
Johnson & Johnson
1 Johnson & Johnson Plaza
New Brunswick, New Jersey 08933
Tel: 732.524.0400
Internet: www.jnj.com

Johnson & Johnson is one of the world's largest and most diversified family of companies, with over 170 operating units in consumer products, professional products and pharmaceuticals. Founded in 1886, JnJ provides its healthcare products globally and encompasses a wealth of opportunity.

Johnson and Johnson offers over 1200 internships in virtually all major business functions for undergraduate, graduates, and MBA candidates. The company prefers applicants with majors in Engineering, Computer Science, Business, Finance, Marketing, Accounting, Human Resources, and the Life Sciences.

Internships give students opportunities to apply academic knowledge in business settings. Their co-op and internship program places qualified students in full- and part-time internship positions within Johnson & Johnson companies.

Internships come with variable, but competitive, stipend amounts. They are available for all three semesters. Deadlines for all three semesters are open. You may apply online at www.jnj.com/careers/interns.htm.

Eli Lilly and Company
Intern Coordinator
Eli Lilly and Company
Corporate Center
Intern Coordinator DC 1029
Indianapolis, Indiana 46285
Tel: 317.276.2000
Internet: www.lilly.com

A major player in the pharmaceutical industry, Lilly's leading product is the anti-depressant drug Prozac. The company also offers a wide range of other products including antibiotics, anti-ulcer agents, growth hormones and animal health products.

The Lilly Internship Program is an integrated program designed to increase awareness of the company and prepare students for future positions. Interns are involved in a wide range of functional areas including marketing, research, finance, human resources and engineering.

Lilly offers over 50 internships in Marketing, Finance, and Engineering over the summer semester. The company prefers candidates with majors in Engineering, Computer Science, Business, Finance, Marketing, Human Resources, and the Life Sciences. MBA students are also attractive candidates.

Internships come with stipends, which are negotiable. Application deadline is December. Send a cover letter and resume online at http://campuszone. lilly.com.

GlaxoSmithKline

Research Triangle Park, NC

Tel: +1.888.825.5249

Internet: www.gsk.com/careers/us-university/university_us_summer.htm

GSK is a leading Big Pharma company and offers internships in all major functional areas in Raleigh, NC and the Greater Philadelphia, PA, area. Internships are offered during the summer semester to currently enrolled students in undergraduate, graduate or Ph.D.-level degree programs. College students need to have, at a minimum, completed their sophomore year of undergraduate studies.

Internship positions are paid, full-time, 10-12 week positions. They typically begin in May and end in August. Application reviews for 2006 begin in January for the following summer. Granted internships are posted online on an ongoing basis, from January to mid-March. Intern salaries are paid hourly and are competitive with the pharmaceutical industry.

GSK also offers an extensive 4- to 8-month co-op education program for students who have completed their sophomore year and who will also receive academic credit for their co-op experience. Co-ops may be completed at either Raleigh or Philadelphia. They are paid as full-time positions on an hourly basis. Rates are competitive within the industry.

Applications are accepted online only, with hard copies specified as unacceptable. The company recommends you browse the site to download documents that provide guidelines to submitting required materials, and review the application submission and review process.

Merck & Co.
Global Headquarters
Merck & Co., Inc.
One Merck Drive
P.O. Box 100
Whitehouse Station, NJ 08889-0100 USA
Tel: 908.423.1000
Internet: www.merck.com

Merck's reach goes way beyond Vioxx. Although the company has internships in most functional areas available via their Web site, a new program combines the Big Pharma experience with an international flavor. Its Canadian division, Merck Frosst Canada Ltd., has teamed up with the Faculty of Pharmaceutical Sciences at the University of British Columbia to create the Graduate Student Internship Program.

Dr. Kishor M. Wasan
National Director, University of British Columbia
Dr. Dale Meisner
National Director, Merck Frosst Canada Ltd.
www.pharmacy.ubc.ca/graduate_programs/graduate_linked_documents/internship_merck2005.pdf

Nuvelo, Inc.
HR Department
Attn: Internship Program Coordinator
201 Industrial Road, Suite 310
San Carlos, CA 94070
Internet: www.nuvelo.com/join/college.html
Fax: 650.517.8001
Email: hr@nuvelo.com (document attachments in RTF or rich text format only)

Though most internship listings are for very large global companies, here is a very small company eager to attract talent. Nuvelo, Inc. has a mere 100 employees and focuses on developing cardiovascular and oncology drugs. The company expects to leverage its discoveries into partnerships and licensing deals with Big Pharma companies to bring these to market via their sales and marketing infrastructure.

Nuvelo is "looking for career-driven self starters." Internships are available for currently enrolled, full-time college students in their junior year.

Visit Vault at **www.vault.com** for insider company profiles, expert advice, career message boards, expert resume reviews, the Vault Job Board and more.

VAULT CAREER LIBRARY   **187**

Applicants with majors in the Life Sciences, Chemistry, Biology, or related disciplines are most attractive. Stipends are included, but not with employee benefits. Applications comprising of a cover letter and resume are accepted either by fax or e-mail at the addresses listed above.

Schering-Plough
University Relations
Schering-Plough
1 Giralda Farms
Madison, New Jersey 07940-1010
Tel: 973.822.7000
Internet: www.sch-plough.com

Schering-Plough is one of the major pharmaceutical companies, producing over-the-counter drugs, prescription drugs, gene-based drugs, and personal care products. The company's workforce diversity program includes programs for minority college students.

Schering-Plough offers over 50 internships in management, sales, and research, which run over the summer semester. The company prefer candidates with majors in Computer Science or the Life Sciences. MBA students are also attractive. Internships include stipends at competitive levels. The deadline for summer internships is December. You may apply online at www.whatdrivesyou.com.

Academic sources of internships

We've included information from two academic programs to show you how extensive dedicated programs can be. Even if you do not attend these institutions, accessing the information on their Web sites might give you ideas on areas of internships you had not previously considered.

Keck Graduate Institute
535 Watson Drive
Claremont, CA 91711
Tel: 909.607.7855
Fax: 909.607.8086
Internet: www.kgi.edu/industry/internships.shtml

Keck Graduate Institute was created with the collaboration of the industry to produce professionals educated in both science and business and socialized to work seamlessly across functional boundaries. Master's Program graduates find positions in the pharmaceutical, biotechnology, medical device and bioagricultural industries. Students are required to take a paid internship during the summer semester between the first and second academic years in a bioscience company.

Keck is a new institution with a new type of program, a Master's in Bioscience (MBS), which is a fully accredited two-year alternative to traditional research and medical training. Because this program is custom-made to the industry's needs, its reach into the industry is as extensive as industry-focused institutions, such as Boston University, discussed below.

Boston University
121 Bay State Road
Boston, MA 02215 USA
Tel: 617.353.2300
Fax: 617.353.9695
Internet: http://management.bu.edu/gpo/hc/internship.asp

Boston University has one of the most extensive internship placement programs. Internships run for 10 weeks over the summer semester between the first and second year of full-time graduate students. Internships of the same scope (about 400 hours) may be completed over either a 12-week period or throughout the academic year for part-time students.

Internship areas include Marketing, Operations Management, Information Systems, Financial Analysis, Strategic Planning, Technology Management, and Accounting. Boston University has placed interns in hospitals, community health centers, biotechnology firms, pharmaceutical organizations, HMOs, long-term care facilities, government agencies, managed care organizations, insurance companies, and consumer organizations.

Even if you are not currently attending BU, checking out their Web site will give you an idea of the scope of placements and projects available. BU students have performed market analyses for new products, created and administered surveys gauging patient satisfaction, and assisted in a strategy assessment of a public welfare system.

Visit Vault at **www.vault.com** for insider company profiles, expert advice, career message boards, expert resume reviews, the Vault Job Board and more.

V/\ULT CAREER LIBRARY   **189**

Trade group sources

PhRMA

Internet: www.phrma.org; www.srpub.phrma.org; or www.genomics.phrma .org.

PhRMA Internships

Ms. Lisa Miles

lmiles@phrma.org

Tel: 202.835.3531

PhRMA, the industry's leading trade association, offers an internship at its Washington, D.C. headquarters.   The PhRMA internship supports the scientific and regulatory affairs divisions of the group. The intern researches issues, drafts policy statements, monitors events, and performs such administrative tasks as maintaining membership rosters.   The internship usually lasts three months, which may be extended to six months on a monthly basis. In 2005, the stipend is $12 per hour for 37.5 hours.

The most attractive candidates will have strong oral and written communication skills, solid organizational and IT skills and demonstrate an interest in science and science policy. College graduates with science majors are preferred but qualified undergraduates will also be considered.

Applications may be sent either by faxing a cover letter, resume, and a writing sample (up to 5 pages) to Ms. Miles at the address listed above or by attaching these documents to an e-mail. Obtain more information by downloading a PDF file at www.pharmacoepi.org/resources/phrma-internship.pdf.

International sources

Most global companies are likely to have international internships, and it is well worth your while to investigate beyond the few examples below. If you are planning your first internship before rising to junior year in college, why not target an international internship for the following summer?   The experience will be invaluable.

Canada

Internet: www.jobpostings.ca/

The Canadian pharmaceutical industry includes brand companies (much like their U.S. counterparts), generics makers, biotech companies, and clinical trial organizations. Again like the U.S., the players are divided into large players with sales and marketing infrastructure and smaller, research-oriented specialty firms, involved mostly in biotech. The industry's large players are clustered in Toronto and Montreal, whereas the biotechs are distributed in Edmonton, Saskatoon, Winnipeg, and Vancouver.

Companies offer internships in the major functional areas and prefer candidates with majors in either the Life Sciences or Business. MBA students are also attractive candidates. Most internships are structured similarly to those in the U.S. and usually run over the summer semester. The following Web sites offer more specific information.

Human Resources Canada, www.hrdc-drhc.gc.ca.

Pharmaceutical Advertising Advisory Board, www.paab.ca.

Canadian Society for Pharmaceutical Sciences, www.ualberta.ca/~csps/.

Canadian Association for Pharmacists, www.pharmacists.ca.

The Canadian Generic Pharmaceutical Association, www.cdma-acfpp.org.

Germany
Type Two Ltd.
Claridge House
29 Barnes High Street
London SW13 9LW | England
Tel: 44 (0) 20 82 82 16 37
Fax: +44 (0) 20 82 82 16 38
Internet: www.type-two.com
VAT Number GB 814605 054
Registered in the UK as a limited company, No. 4605523

This is an internship from a British pharmaceutical industry management consultancy for a project in Frankfurt, Germany. The company has a global reach and counts the leading global companies as its clients.

This internship focuses on providing assistance to the client company in creating a sourcing strategy for Asia. The intern's responsibilities include gathering information, performing analyses within a team context, offering conclusions, suggesting alternative solutions to client problems, and attending project meetings.

Applicants with majors in business, science, or medical backgrounds are most attractive. All applicants should be fluent in English, with German fluency a plus. The company notes also that team skills, initiative, flexibility and solid analytical skills are essential.

The internship was offered for 12 weeks from September to November, 2005, but is not unlikely that it will be offered in subsequent years. The internship comes with a stipend, which is competitive within the industry.

Applicants may send a cover letter and resume via email to Till Erdmann at ter@type-two.com.

This link, www.uni-koeln.de/allgemeines/stellenangebote/typetwo2.pdf from a German site, provides additional context.

Australia
R&D Advisory Services
rdadvisory@sd.qld.gov.au
Tel: +61 7 3227 7211
Internet: www.sdi.qld.gov.au/dsdweb/v3/ documents/objdirctrled/nonsecure/pdf
The Australian government has recently completed an analysis of its pharmaceutical and biotech industries and has invested over $1M to establish internship programs for science, engineering, and technology undergraduate students. Applicants with those majors are most attractive.

With global companies sourcing components of drug development - from clinical trials to manufacturing facilities - in economies with lower costs than in the U.S., many countries have commissioned such studies in order to better understand global trends and connect them to competitive advantages they have, which in turn will help develop their own local industries. One advantage Australia has is that it is part of the English-speaking world; thus, interns from the U.S. can participate in Australian programs relatively seamlessly.

Goals of the programs include encouraging students to major in the sciences (or switch to a science major), helping them break into the industry (via internships), and attracting the local population into staff positions within the industry.

Internships include a stipend, which is competitive within the industry. Application deadline is November. For complete details, download the Guidelines for Applicants or contact R&D Advisory Services on rdadvisory@sd.qld.gov.au or +61 7 3227 7211.

Pharma Glossary

Abbreviated new drug application (ANDA) - The application filed for generic drugs. It's substantially shorter than the New Drug Application (NDA) required for new prescription drugs, because generics need only to prove that they're the bioequivalents of the branded drugs they replicate.

Agonist - A drug that promotes certain kinds of cellular activity by binding to a cell's receptor.

Amino acids - Building blocks of proteins, including alanine, aspartic acid, glutamic acid, and additional compounds.

Anesthetic - A drug used to produce unconsciousness or to numb a local area of the body.

Antagonist - A drug that prevents certain types of cellular reactions by blocking substances from binding to a cell's receptor.

Antibody - A protein produced by certain types of white blood cells to deactivate foreign proteins.

Antigen - Any substance that induces a body's immune response.

Antispasmodic - A compound designed to reduce unwanted muscular contractions in the gastrointestinal tract.

Autoimmune disease - A condition, such as multiple sclerosis, where the body produces antibodies against its own tissues.

Bioavailability - The percentage of a drug's active ingredient that reaches a patient's bloodstream and body tissues.

Bioinformatics - A system whereby biological information is collected, stored, and accessed via computers and similar electronic media.

Biological - A medicinal preparation made from living organisms or their byproducts. Vaccines, antigens, serums, and plasmas are examples of biologicals.

Breakthrough drug - A compound whose chemical composition or mode of action is significantly different than that of existing drugs, representing a major therapeutic advance.

Bronchodilator - A drug used to widen the bronchioles (tubular extensions within the lungs) to aid in respiration.

Visit Vault at **www.vault.com** for insider company profiles, expert advice, career message boards, expert resume reviews, the Vault Job Board and more.

VAULT CAREER LIBRARY   **193**

Chemotherapy drugs - Drugs used to treat cancers.

Chromosomes - Microscopic threadlike components in the nucleus of a cell that carry hereditary information in the form of genes.

Clinical trials - Tests through which experimental drugs are administered to humans to determine their safety and efficacy.

Clotting factors - Proteins involved in the normal clotting of blood.

Combination therapy - The use of two or more drugs that together have greater therapeutic power in treating illness and diseases than either used alone.

Corticosteroids - Natural steroid hormones secreted by the adrenal glands, or synthetic copies used to treat inflammation and other conditions.

Deoxyribonucleic acid (DNA) - The basic molecule that contains genetic information for most living systems. The DNA molecule consists of four nucleotide bases (adenine, cytosine, guanine, and thymine) and a sugar-phosphate frame arranged in two connected strands, forming a double helix.

Diagnosis-related groups (DRGs) - A classification system by which the U.S. government reimburses hospitals on a fixed-fee basis for care provided to Medicare beneficiaries.

Enzyme - A protein that controls chemical reactions in the human body.

Ethical drugs - Medicines requiring a doctor's prescription.

Formulary - A select list of drugs that a healthcare insurer has approved for reimbursement.

Gene - The basic determinant of heredity, genes are chromosomal segments that direct the syntheses of proteins and conduct other molecular regulatory functions.

Genomics - The study of genes and their functions, including mapping genes within the genome, identifying their nucleic acid structures, and investigating their functions.

Generic drug - A compound that contains the same active ingredients as a branded drug. A company cannot market a generic version of a rival's branded product until its patent expires.

Growth factors - Proteins responsible for regulating cell proliferation, function, and differentiation.

Health maintenance organization (HMO) - A healthcare plan that offers subscribers unlimited access to comprehensive medical services from a select list of providers. Subscribers prepay fixed fees to belong.

Hormone - A chemical produced by a gland and released in the bloodstream.

Immunomodulator - A drug that attempts to modify the immune system.

Investigational new drug (IND) - An experimental new compound that has successfully completed animal studies and has been approved by the Food and Drug Administration (FDA) to proceed to human trials.

Managed care - A supervised system of financing and providing healthcare services for a defined population group. HMOs are currently the most popular form of managed care.

Medicaid - A joint U.S. federal/state program that provides medical services to low-income patients. Medicaid also pays for nursing home services for indigent elderly patients.

Medicare - A federally funded U.S. national health insurance program for persons aged 65 and older, and for all disabled persons, regardless of income.

Neurotransmitter - A compound designed to act upon the transfer of electrical impulses in the nervous system.

Monoclonal antibodies - Large protein molecules produced by white blood cells, which seek out and destroy harmful foreign substances.

New drug application (NDA) - The formal filing that drugmakers submit to the FDA for approval to market new drugs. The document must contain clinical evidence of the compound's safety and efficacy.

Orphan drug - A drug designed to treat rare diseases afflicting a relatively small patient population. The U.S. government gives drugmakers special incentives to encourage the development of such drugs.

Outcomes management - Evaluations of the relative success and cost-efficiency of various medical products and services. Outcomes management is typically employed by HMOs and other managed care providers to justify the choice or coverage of a particular type of therapy. Pharmaceutical companies are also keenly interested in data obtained from outcomes management for marketing purposes and to determine future R&D directions.

Over-the-counter (OTC) drugs - Compounds sold in pharmacies and other outlets without need of a prescription. Also referred to as proprietary medications.

Visit Vault at www.vault.com for insider company profiles, expert advice, career message boards, expert resume reviews, the Vault Job Board and more.

VAULT CAREER LIBRARY   195

Pharmacogenomics - The study of how an individual's genetic composition affects the response to drugs. It combines traditional pharmaceutical sciences such as biochemistry with the knowledge of genes, proteins, and single nucleotide polymorphisms.

Pharmacokinetics - Analysis of a drug's absorption and distribution in the body, its chemical changes in the body, and how it is stored and eliminated from the body.

Recombinant DNA technology - The process of creating new DNA by combining components of DNA from different organisms. Usually, the new DNA is incorporated into therapeutic substances.

Therapeutic substitution - A policy that some managed care organizations employ to substitute less expensive drugs for more expensive ones in the same therapeutic class, even though the drugs use different modes of action.

Treatment IND - An FDA program that allows experimental drugs (known as "investigational new drugs") that treat life-threatening diseases to be made commercially available to very sick patients before the drugs obtain formal FDA approval.

Source: *Standard & Poor's Industry Surveys*

About the Author

Carole S. Moussalli

Ms. Moussalli is an author, teacher, and consultant. Most recently, she has been a contributing author to the International Directory of Business Biographies, for which she profiled C-level executives in the U.S. and South Korea. She has taught Global Business Communication to pre-MBA students at Korea University. As a consultant, Ms. Moussalli has provided global product launch support and managed the development of sales training and other professional development programs for major biopharmaceutical companies.

Ms. Moussalli earned her MBA from Columbia Business School in 2003 with a focus in marketing and general management. She also completed graduate coursework in psychology at Harvard University and earned an MS in Chemistry from the University of North Carolina and a BA in Chemistry from Manhattanville College.